At Issue

Does Capital Punishment
Deter Crime?

Other Books in the At Issue Series:

At Issue

Does Capital Punishment Deter Crime?

Amy Marcaccio Keyzer, Book Editor

GREENHAVEN PRESS
An imprint of Thomson Gale, a part of The Thomson Corporation

Detroit • New York • San Francisco • New Haven, Conn. • Waterville, Maine • London

Christine Nasso, *Publisher*
Elizabeth Des Chenes, *Managing Editor*

© 2007 The Gale Group.

For more information, contact:
Greenhaven Press
27500 Drake Rd.
Farmington Hills, MI 48331-3535
Or you can visit our Internet site at http://www.gale.com

LIBRARY OF CONGRESS CATALOGING-IN-PUBLICATION DATA

Does capital punishment deter crime? / Amy Marcaccio Keyzer, book editor.
   p. cm. -- (At issue)
  Includes bibliographical references and index.
  ISBN-13: 978-0-7377-3675-5 (hardcover)
  ISBN-13: 978-0-7377-3676-2 (pbk.)
  1. Capital punishment--United States. 2. Punishment in crime deterrence--United States. I. Keyzer, Amy Marcaccio.
  HV8699.U5D646 2008
  364.660973--dc22

2007028827

ISBN-10: 0-7377-3675-5 (hardcover)
ISBN-10: 0-7377-3676-3 (pbk.)

Printed in the United States of America
10 9 8 7 6 5 4 3 2 1

Contents

Introduction

On December 30, 2006, the U.S.-backed, Shi'ite-led Iraqi government executed former Iraqi dictator Saddam Hussein on the major Muslim holiday of Eid al-Adha, the Feast of the Sacrifice. Despite the heinous crimes Saddam committed against his own people over the years, the timing and the undignified manner of the Sunni tyrant's hanging death, which was broadcast to the world via an image captured by a covert camera phone, did little to squelch the violence in Iraq or deter others from following in his footsteps. Rather, sectarian strife escalated as Shi'ite and Sunni Muslims continued to fight, killing civilians and militants in bombings across the country. *Time* correspondent Aparisim Ghosh noted, "Like rulers before him, Saddam exploited the Shi'ite-Sunni divide for his own purposes. The scenes from his execution suggest Iraq's new rulers are not all that different."

Iraq shares the company of such countries as Iran, Pakistan, China, Singapore, Saudi Arabia, and Somalia in its use of capital punishment, but among industrialized Western democracies, the United States is the only nation that still implements the death penalty. According to Amnesty International, as of February 2007, a total of 128 countries have abolished the death penalty in law or practice, with 88 countries and territories prohibiting it for all crimes. Amnesty International also reports that in 2005, 94 percent of all known executions, estimated to be at least 2,148 people, took place in China, Iran, Saudi Arabia, and the United States.

The United States has long held a role of moral leadership in the world, but some believe that the U.S. stance on capital punishment may be endangering its international image as a protector of human rights. Most of the international community has called for the limitation, if not outright abolition, of the death penalty. The European Union considers it "a cruel and unusual punishment" that "provides no added value in terms of deterrence." Although he understood the Iraqi people's desire for justice in the case of Saddam Hussein, United Nations Special Representative Ashraf Qazi reiterated that "the United Nations remains opposed to capital punishment, even in the case of war crimes, crimes against humanity and genocide."

Following the terrorist attacks of September 11, 2001, Americans became more aware of national security issues and law enforcement tools that would help prevent such atrocities from happening again. One such tool is the death penalty. Supporters maintain that it sends a strong deterrent message to those who would harm civilians, thus saving lives and keeping the nation safer. On the other side, opponents point to the willingness of terrorists to commit suicide bombings in order to kill innocent people and achieve perceived martyrdom. These particular murderers do not fear death, so the death penalty is ineffective in deterring these would-be killers. However, law professor Joanna Shepherd finds that current research and examples suggest some terrorists may be influenced by capital punishment. In her 2004 testimony before the U.S. House Judiciary Committee, she contended: "That many potential perpetrators view execution as worse than life imprisonment confirms why the existence of the death penalty would deter at least a few from committing murder."

Proponents of capital punishment have long argued that it deters potential murderers from committing the ultimate crime and is more effective than a "life without parole" prison sentence. In the 1970s, the statistical research of economist Isaac Ehrlich led Ehrlich to estimate that each execution resulted in approximately seven or eight fewer murders. More recent deterrence studies even claim that such factors as lengthy waits on death row and death sentence commutations can reduce the deterrent impact of the death penalty, causing murder rates to increase.

Opponents of capital punishment assert that state-sponsored executions create a brutalization effect in society, increasing the violent tendencies of criminals and devaluing human life. Death penalty critics and experts have challenged the findings of modern deterrence research, citing lack of scientific standards. Finding no convincing evidence that executions deter others from committing murder, lawyer and author Scott Turow noted in 2003, "Illinois, which has a death penalty, has a higher murder rate than the neighboring state of Michigan, which has no capital punishment but roughly the same racial makeup, income levels, and population distribution between cities and rural areas." Further, the 2004 FBI Uniform Crime Report revealed that the South, which accounts for over 80 percent of executions, had the highest murder rate in the United States, whereas the Northeast, with less than 1 percent of executions, had the lowest.

The American Civil Liberties Union finds another flaw in the deterrence argument, emphasizing, "People commit murders largely in the heat of passion, and/or under the influence of alcohol or drugs, giving little thought to the possible consequences of their acts. The few murderers who plan their crimes beforehand—for example, professional executioners—intend and expect to avoid punishment altogether by not getting caught."

Retributive justice often walks hand-in-hand with deterrence in a seemingly logical relationship, akin to killing the proverbial two birds with one stone. The execution of a person who has committed a particularly brutal crime, so the reasoning goes, not only represents the community's moral outrage at the act, but also serves as a warning to others, preventing similar crimes. In a 2001 essay, professor of religion and philosophy J. Daryl Charles expressed the view that a civilized culture is morally obliged to impose the death penalty. According to Charles, "A society unwilling to direct retributive justice toward those who murder in cold blood is a society that has deserted its responsibility to uphold the unique value of human life."

Cardinal Roger Mahony, Archbishop of Los Angeles, speaking in 2000 to the National Press Club, suggested another way of looking at the "logic" of deterrence and retribution. "I do not believe that society is made safer, that our communities are made whole, or that our social fabric is strengthened, by killing those who kill others," he stated. "Instead, the death penalty perpetuates an insidious cycle of violence that, in the end, diminishes all of us. . . . The answer to violence cannot be more violence."

Arguments for and against capital punishment's ability to deter crime continue to ferment. While some believe fervently that the death penalty is just and effective, others echo Mohandas Gandhi's sentiment that "An eye for an eye makes the whole world blind." Whether the United States retains the death penalty may ultimately be linked to pressure from the international community or the desire for greater cooperation in the global war on terror, rather than internal debate. The authors whose works are presented in *At Issue: Does Capital Punishment Deter Crime?* provide a broad range of legal, moral, and scientific perspectives on the deterrent aspect of the most extreme punishment.

Consistent and Swift Application of the Death Penalty Reduces Murder Rates

Wesley Lowe

Wesley Lowe is a fantasy novelist and an advocate of capital punishment.

Despite widespread support for capital punishment in the United States, the death penalty has become a controversial issue. Abolitionists claim that the fear of death does not deter potential criminals, yet policemen are able to capture perpetrators at gunpoint precisely because criminals fear lethal force. Between 1965 and 1980, a period during which few executions took place (and with executions temporarily suspended between 1972 and 1976), the number of annual murders in the United States increased by 131 percent. After capital punishment resumed more aggressively, with executions averaging 71 per year from 1995 to 2000, a dramatic decrease was seen in the homicide rate. If the death penalty were applied consistently, efficiently, and swiftly, it would more effectively deter murder.

When asked in a straight forward sense—"Do you support the death penalty for murder?" polls show very few countries where the public clearly opposes it. According to such polls, around 70% of the American people support the Death Penalty. Between 60% and 70% of Canadians want the Death Penalty reinstated in Canada. In Britain, two-thirds and three-quarters of the population favors the Death Penalty. In France, clear majorities continue to back the Death Penalty long after it was abolished in 1981. In the U.S., during the temporary suspension on capital punishment from 1972–1976, the murder rate doubled. With the increased use of the Death Penalty, the murder rate is now at its lowest level in the US since 1966. . . .

Putting to death people judged to have committed certain extremely heinous crimes is a practice of ancient standing, but in the United States in the latter half of the twentieth century, it has become a very controversial issue. Changing views on this difficult issue and many legal challenges to capital punishment working their way through the courts resulted in a halt to executions in the United States in 1967. Eventually, the Supreme Court placed a moratorium on capital punishment in 1972 but later upheld it in 1977, with certain conditions.

My state of New York is a state that practiced capital punishment since its colonial days, then abolished it in 1965. But now, as of September 1, 1995, the death penalty is back on the books in accordance to Governor Pataki's campaign promise. As a staunch supporter of the death penalty, I consider this to be a good thing for my state and its citizens.

Indeed, restoring capital punishment is the will of the people, yet many voices are raised against it. Heated public debate centers on questions of deterrence, public safety, sentencing equity, and the execution of innocents, among others. I have listened and read the arguments opposing the death penalty and I find that they are not at all convincing. Here's why.

The Deterrent Effect of Capital Punishment

One argument states that the death penalty does not deter murder. Dismissing capital punishment on that basis requires us to eliminate all prisons as well because they do not seem to be any more effective in the deterrence of crime.

Others say that states which do have the death penalty have higher crime rates than those that don't, that a more severe punishment only inspires more severe crimes. I must point out that every state in the union is different. These differences include the populations, number of cities, and yes, the crime rates. Strongly urbanized states are more likely to have higher crime rates than states that are more rural, such as those that lack capital punishment. The states that have capital punishment are compelled to have it due to their higher crime rates, not the other way around.

Abolitionists also hold the notion that criminals do not fear death because they do not take time to think about the consequences of their acts. If that were true, then I wonder how police officers manage to arrest criminals without killing them. When a policeman holds a criminal at gunpoint and tells him to get on the ground, the criminal will comply fully in the vast majority of these cases. Why would they do that unless they were afraid of the lethal power of the gun? It is because regardless of what abolitionists claim, criminals are not immune to fear! It is a common misconception to believe that fear is a thought process that has to be worked out with a piece of paper. It's not! It is an instinct that automatically kicks in when one is faced with lethal force! The examples below should confirm that point.

More Executions, Fewer Murders

During the temporary suspension on capital punishment from 1972–1976, researchers gathered murder statistics across the country. In 1960, there were 56 executions in the USA and 9,140 murders. By 1964, when there were only 15 executions, the number of murders had risen to 9,250. In 1969, there were no executions and 14,590 murders, and 1975, after six more years without executions, 20,510 murders occurred rising to 23,040 in 1980 after only two executions since 1976. In summary, between 1965 and 1980, the number of annual murders in the United States skyrocketed from 9,960 to 23,040, a 131 percent increase. The murder rate—homicides per 100,000 persons—doubled from 5.1 to 10.2. So the number of murders grew as the number of executions shrank. Researcher Karl Spence of Texas A&M University said:

> While some [death penalty] abolitionists try to face down the results of their disastrous experiment and still argue to the contrary, the ... [data] concludes that a substantial deterrent effect has been observed. ... In six months, more Americans are murdered than have been killed by execution in this entire century. ... Until we begin to fight crime in earnest [by using the death penalty], every person who dies at a criminal's hands is a victim of our inaction.

Notes Dudley Sharp of the criminal-justice reform group Justice for All:

> From 1995 to 2000, executions averaged 71 per year, a 21,000 percent increase over the 1966–1980 period. The murder rate dropped from a high of 10.2 (per 100,000) in 1980 to 5.7 in 1999–a 44 percent reduction. The murder rate is now at its lowest level since 1966. ...

And that's not all.

If the death penalty were just as consistent, lethal, and as unstoppable as the AIDS virus, criminals would actually have reason to back down.

The most striking protection of innocent life has been seen in Texas, which executes more murderers than any other state. According to JFA (Justice for All), the Texas murder rate in 1991 was 15.3 per 100,000. By 1999, it had fallen to 6.1—a drop of 60 percent. Within Texas, the most aggressive death penalty prosecutions are in Harris County (the Houston area). Since the resumption of executions in 1982, the annual number of Harris County murders has plummeted from 701 to 241—a 72 percent decrease.

Swift and Certain Justice Deters Crime

In 1997, in the *Atlantic*, reporter Robert Kaplan remarked that "Democratic South Africa has become one of the most violent places on earth that are not war zones. The murder rate is six times that in the United States, five times that in Russia. There are private security guards for every policeman." Yet, South African officials still insist that the death penalty won't do a thing to reduce the murder rate. The *New York Times* magazine carried a story on the epidemic of rapes of children in the country:

> South Africa may have the highest incidence of reported rape in the world—120.6 rapes for every 100,000 women in 1997, compared with 71 in the US in 1996.

One reason for the increase in attacks on young children is that the rapists think they are less likely to have AIDS since they know that AIDS itself has skyrocketed in Nelson Mandela's "earthly paradise." Think about that. Those rapists are less likely to attack grown women because they fear the lethal consequences of AIDS. This demonstrates that violent criminals are indeed capable of being deterred by lethal consequences for their actions because they are not immune to fear. If the death penalty were just as consistent, lethal, and as unstoppable as the AIDS virus, criminals would actually have reason to back down. Given the evidence, there is no logical reason to believe otherwise.

Edward Koch, former mayor of New York City, said:

> Had the death penalty been a real possibility in the minds of . . . murderers, they might well have stayed their hand. They might have shown moral awareness before their victims died. . . . Consider the tragic death of Rosa Velez, who happened to be home when a man named Luis Vera burglarized her apartment in Brooklyn. "Yeah, I shot her," Vera admitted. ". . . and I knew I wouldn't go to the chair."

Abolitionists will claim that most studies show that the death penalty has no effect on the murder rate at all. But that's only because those studies have been focused on inconsistent executions. Capital punishment, like all other applications, must be used consistently in order to be effective. However, the death penalty hasn't been used consistently in the USA for decades, so abolitionists have been able to establish the delusion that it doesn't deter at all to rationalize their fallacious arguments. But the evidence shows that whenever capital punishment is applied consistently or against a small murder rate it has always been followed by a decrease in murder. I have yet to see an example on how the death penalty has failed to reduce the murder rate under those conditions.

Rows and rows of Thuggees were left hanging from the gallows along the roads by the dozens. This not only established a zero recidivism rate, but it also greatly discouraged new membership into the cult.

So capital punishment is very capable of deterring murder if we allow it to, but our legal system is so slow and inefficient, criminals are able to stay several steps ahead of us and gain leeway through our lenience. Several reforms must be made in our justice system so the death penalty can cause a positive effect.

Historical Evidence of Deterrence

There are many examples of how the death penalty deters murder. . . . But here is an example of how the use of consistent executions have dramatically improved certain societies.

In the 1800s, in English-occupied India, there was one of the worst gangs of murdering thieves the world has ever known, the Indian hoodlum band known as the Thuggees. Through the course of their existence, dating back to the 1550s, the Thuggees were credited with murdering more than

2,000,000 people, mostly wealthy travelers. The killer secret society plagued India for more than 350 years. The Thuggees traveled in gangs, sometimes disguised as poor beggars or religious mendicants. Sometimes they wore the garb of rich merchants to get closer to unsuspecting victims. One of their principles was never to spill blood, so they always strangled their victims. Each member was required to kill at least once a year in order to maintain membership in the cult. But they killed in the name of religion. The deaths were conceived of as human sacrifices to Kali, the bloodthirsty Hindustani goddess of destruction. It came to pass that the Thuggees began to kill using pickaxes and knives. According to legend, the Thuggees believed that Kali devoured the bodies of their victims. The story goes that once a member of the society hid behind a tree in order to spy on the goddess. The angry goddess punished the Thuggees by making them bury their victims from then on.

Speedy Executions Eliminate Cult

The ruling British government worked very hard to stop the Thuggee religion and its murderous practices. Between 1829 and 1848, the British managed to suppress the Thuggees by means of mass arrests and speedy executions. Indeed, rows and rows of Thuggees were left hanging from the gallows along the roads by the dozens. This not only established a zero recidivism rate, but it also greatly discouraged new membership into the cult. The most lethal practitioner of the cult of Thuggee was Buhram. At his trial it was established that he had murdered 931 people between 1790 and 1840. All had been strangled with his waistcloth. Burham was executed in 1840. Appropriately enough, he was hanged until he strangled. In 1832, the Agent to the Governor-General of India, F. C. Smith, had this to say about the Thugees and their deeds:

> I have never heard of such atrocities, or presided over such trials, such cold-blooded murders, such heart-rending scenes

of distress and misery; such base ingratitude; such a total abandonment of the very principle which binds man to man; which softens the heart and elevates mankind above the brute creation . . . mercy to such wretches would be the extreme of cruelty to mankind . . . blood for blood.

In 1882, the British government deemed the problem solved with the hanging death of the last known Thuggee. Good riddance.

The Deterrent Effect of the Death Penalty Is a Myth

Rev. Jesse L. Jackson Sr., Jesse L. Jackson Jr., and Bruce Shapiro

Rev. Jesse L. Jackson Sr. is the founder and president of the Rainbow/PUSH Coalition and a leading figure in civil rights and politics. Jesse L. Jackson Jr. has represented the Second District of Illinois in the United States Congress since 1995. Bruce Shapiro is a contributing editor at the Nation *and a national correspondent for Salon.com, and he has written extensively on civil liberties and human rights.*

Politicians often echo the popular belief that capital punishment deters criminals from murdering, creating a safer society. However, many law enforcement officials disagree with this logic. Throughout history, other voices have proclaimed that the death penalty actually increases the violent tendencies of criminals because it devalues human life. Although statistical studies on capital punishment and deterrence from the 1970s indicate that executions prevent homicides, more recent studies refute this conclusion. Most would-be murderers are not rational and do not take into consideration the state in which they commit their crimes or the penalty for their actions. Life imprisonment can protect lives as effectively as capital punishment if society is concerned about a killer murdering again. Politicians who want to be seen as tough on crime perpetuate the deterrence myth.

Rev. Jesse L. Jackson Sr., Jessie L. Jackson Jr., and Bruce Shapiro, *Legal Lynching: The Death Penalty and America's Future*. New York: The New Press, 2001. Copyright © 2001 by Rev. Jesse L. Jackson Sr., Representative Jesse L. Jackson Jr., Bruce Shapiro. All rights reserved. Reproduced by permission.

In the close and contentious presidential campaign of 2000, candidates Al Gore and George W. Bush didn't agree on much. They fought over taxes, over education, over affirmative action, over oil drilling.

But one curious point of agreement emerged in the final presidential debate, on October 19, 2000. It was not a reporter who asked the revealing question but an audience member, Leo Anderson. Mr. Anderson pointed out how in a debate one week earlier, Governor Bush seemed to "overly enjoy" invoking the death penalty during a discussion of hate crimes and the murder of James Byrd, an African-American man dragged to death in Texas. "Are you really, really proud of the fact that Texas is number one in executions?" Anderson asked.

Well, no, replied the Texas governor. "If you think I was proud of it, I think you misread me." But then he added: "I think the reason to support the death penalty is because it saves other people's lives." Gore, clearly not wanting to be outdone in the law-and-order department, chimed in with the same assertion: "It's a deterrence."

"It saves other people's lives." "It's a deterrence." Those simple phrases, articulated by two presidential candidates across wide gulfs of party and philosophy, express the most commonly held view of capital punishment's value. Killing killers prevents crime. The death penalty makes a safer society.

There is only one problem with this logic: It isn't true.

Challenging the Logic of Deterrence

Whatever the philosophical justifications might be for capital punishment, deterring crime isn't among them. Just ask the nation's top law enforcement officials. A 1995 poll by Hart Research Associates found that just 1 percent of the nation's police chiefs believe the death penalty significantly reduces the number of homicides. Then-Attorney General Janet Reno, a death-penalty supporter whose Justice Department crafted laws making it far harder for death-row inmates to appeal

their sentences, put it this way in 1999: "I have inqu
most of my adult life about studies that might show th_ _____
penalty is a deterrent. And I have not seen any research that
would substantiate that point."

The belief that the severity of execution discourages others
from wrongdoing is probably as old as the death penalty itself.
As long ago as 1566, Pope Pius V in his Roman Catechism declared that the death penalty, along with other punishments,
gives "security to life by repressing outrage and violence." In
colonial America, Protestant ministers routinely delivered
public sermons on the eve of executions extolling the virtue of
hanging's example. In 1790, New Haven, Connecticut, minister James Dana delivered one such sermon—entitled simply
"The Aims of Capital Punishment"—three hours before the
hanging of James Mountain, a free black man convicted of
raping a white teenage girl. The purpose of capital punishment, Dana declared, was both "to rid the state of a present
nuisance" and particularly "to strike terror into the minds of
undetected criminals, youth and all persons watching." The
execution of Mountain would be "a spectacle to the world, a
warning to the vicious."

---

*By devaluing human life and sanctioning an official
policy of vengeance, the death penalty actually increased
the violence in society and, hence, the murder rate.*

Yet by the time of Dana's sermon, influential voices were
already challenging the logic of deterrence, beginning with
[Italian economist and criminologist Cesare] Beccaria, who
declared capital punishment not just morally wrong but "inef-
fectual." Far from reducing crime, Beccaria argued, execution
actually creates it, raising the stakes for lawbreakers, making
desperate individuals only more desperate, and setting an example of brutality:

21

The worse the ill that confronts them, the more men are driven to evade it. The very savagery of punishment has this effect, and to avoid the penalty for one crime they have already committed, men commit other crimes. Countries and times in which punishments have been the most savage have always been those of the bloodiest and most inhuman acts, inasmuch as the spirit of ferocity which guided the hand of the lawgiver also guided the hand of the parricide and cutthroat.

In 1825, attorney and politician Edward Livingstone—who in a career of astonishing breadth represented both New York and Louisiana in Congress, was elected mayor of New York City, and ultimately appointed secretary of state by [President] Andrew Jackson—proposed a model Louisiana criminal code that completely abolished capital punishment. In terms that sound utterly contemporary to our ears, he challenged his opponents to make their best case:

> By your own account, all nations, since the first institution of society, have practiced it, but you yourselves must acknowlege, without success. All we ask, then, is that you abandon an experiment which has for five or six thousand years been progressing under the variety of forms which cruel ingenuity could invent; and which in all ages, under all governments, has been found wanting. . . . You have made your experiment . . . it was found often fatal to the innocent, and it frequently permitted the guilty to escape. . . . Tortures were superadded, which nothing but the intelligence of a fiend could invent; yet there was no diminution of crime.

The Death Penalty Increases Violence

A few years later, in the 1840s, Robert Rantoul, a Massachusetts state representative, conducted the first systematic study of deterrence and came to the conclusion that it didn't work. He believed that by devaluing human life and sanctioning an official policy of vengeance, the death penalty actually increased the violence in society and, hence, the murder rate.

Rantoul addressed his colleagues in the state legislature in an 1846 debate on public executions, presenting evidence that disputed his opponents' claims of deterrence. He explained that in nations such as England and France, where the proportion of executions to convictions was much smaller than in Massachusetts, and also much smaller than the rate in those countries 50 years before, the murder rate was actually decreasing. He had also studied the murder and execution rates in Belgium and noted that the three years in which there were more than 50 executions a year were followed by the three most murderous years in Belgium's history.

With the advent of social science and modern statistical methods, scholars looked anew at the death-penalty deterrence factor. Early in the twentieth century, American researchers compared homicide rates in states that had abolished the death penalty to rates in neighboring states that continued to use capital punishment. Five decades of research across the country failed to show a higher murder rate in states that had abolished the death penalty.

A number of researchers also took a look at states that had either abolished the death penalty or had reinstated its use after a period of abolition. In startling contradiction to what deterrence theory predicts, these studies found that murder rates were stable; they did not rise after a state stopped using capital punishment, nor did they decline when a state reintroduced capital punishment. In the late 1950s, sociologist Thorsten Sellin studied five groups of similar states in the Midwest and New England, with each group including at least one state that used the death penalty while the others did not. Sellin found that the average homicide rate in these states between 1940 and 1955 was in no way related to whether or not the state sanctioned execution as a punishment.

Deterrence Makes a Comeback in the 1970s

Yet by the late 1970s deterrence arguments were making a comeback. The decade from 1967 to 1977 in which no executions were carried out in the United States coincided with a widespread rise in crime; although scholars differed (and still differ) [as of 2001] about the reasons for that rise, politicians and policymakers seized upon the death penalty as a panacea for public fear, after *Furman v. Georgia* in 1972, rushing through new laws they hoped would meet with Supreme Court approval. Capital punishment was proposed as a deterrent to everything from serial-sexual predators to presidential assassinations.

Against this backdrop, Isaac Ehrlich's 1975 study "The Deterrent Effect of Capital Punishment: A Question of Life and Death" landed like a bombshell. Ehrlich analyzed annual national homicide and execution rates from 1933 until 1970. Using computerized statistical methods and controlling for a number of other factors that contribute to the homicide rate—such as unemployment, age distribution, and per capita income—Ehrlich found a deterrent factor. Based on his numbers, Ehrlich boldly estimated that each execution deterred approximately eight homicides—a figure seized upon immediately by death-penalty advocates.

Gilmore's execution didn't deter potential killers; several feet of snow and bitter wind chills did.

But in the years that followed, numerous scientists failed to replicate Ehrlich's results, and his methods are now considered profoundly suspect. For example, researchers using an econometric model, a newer and more powerful statistical procedure, concluded that Ehrlich's data did not support his results. Another researcher refined Ehrlich's social and economic controls on poverty, educational levels, and family structures. These refinements appeared to account for the "deterrent factor" that Ehrlich had supposedly found. Still other analysts showed that by lumping together statistics from all of the states, he masked significant differences in rates among states, specifically between states maintaining the death penalty and those that had abolished capital punishment.

A New Generation of Research

Ehrlich's research, in any event, was entirely historical. Utah's execution of Gary Gilmore in 1977 and the growing number of executions that followed inspired a new generation of contemporary research. Psychology professor Sam McFarland saw these first executions as his opportunity to test the claim of death-penalty supporters that the fear of receiving the ultimate sanction deterred would-be criminals from committing murder. The first four executions after reinstitution occurred between 1977 and 1981. McFarland analyzed the weekly homicide rates in the months following these executions and found that in the two weeks following Gilmore's execution, national homicide rates were significantly below average. However, the next three executions had no perceptible effect on the murder rate.

A less thorough researcher might have concluded that the results confirmed a deterrent factor that was dependent on public awareness, but McFarland searched for other factors. He determined that Gilmore's execution coincided with some of the worst winter weather to hit the eastern half of the country in years. Blizzards blanketed the East Coast as far south as Georgia and Alabama, and the mercury plunged far below normal in the January weeks immediately after Gilmore's execution.

When he examined his data regionally, McFarland found a sharp drop in homicides in the Northeast and the South during the exceptionally inclement period, but in western states experiencing normal weather patterns, homicide rates were at their usual levels. Gilmore's execution didn't deter potential killers; several feet of snow and bitter wind chills did.

Larger-scale studies since have deflated even further any claims that capital punishment deters crime. William C. Bailey, a sociologist at Cleveland State University, has scoured crime statistics for evidence that execution discourages crime ever since the mid-1970s. Bailey's work has ranged from the historic (Chicago homicides and executions in the 1920s) to the contemporary (killings of police officers from the 1970s onward). After breaking down figures into every conceivable category from serial killing to domestic violence, and examining homicides that fall short of first-degree murder as well, Bailey reached this conclusion:

> Neither economists nor sociologists, nor persons from any other discipline (law, psychology, engineering, etc.) have produced credible evidence of a significant deterrent for capital punishment. . . . The evidence remains "clear and abundant" that, as practiced in the United States, capital punishment is not more effective than imprisonment in reducing murder.

Bailey is not alone in his devastating conclusion about the death penalty's irrelevance as a deterrent. In 1999 the scholarly journal *Crime and Delinquency* examined more than a decade of executions in George W. Bush's Texas, and found "no evidence of a deterrent effect." Other research has reached the same conclusion, most notably a 1997 study of crime in more than 500 counties nationwide.

Murderers Not Rational

Deterrence theory is predicated on the seemingly common-sense notion that the possibility of receiving the death penalty will deter would-be killers, whereas the possibility of receiving a sentence of life in prison without possibility of parole will not. If murderers were rational people educated in the laws of the states in which they live, the theory might have some weight. For criminals to be deterred by the penalty, they must know the possible penalties in the state in which they commit their crimes and, in addition, must rationally weigh the risks and benefits of their actions.

Most homicides, however, are unplanned, impulsive acts by one person against another. The emotionally charged environment in which these crimes take place does not suggest a cool, calculating murderer weighing his options.

If a murderer were to sit down to calculate the odds of being punished for a premeditated act of violence, this is what he would have to consider. In the United States, the death penalty is handed down for only about 1 out of every 100 homicides. In capital cases, the rate is higher, but it is still only 6 to 15 per 100 offenses (depending on the state), and of those sentenced, only 6 per 100 are executed. With these odds, the threat of being killed by the planned victim or in a confrontation with police is a much more realistic threat than the distant and abstract possibility of execution. But even those more immediate threats have yet to eliminate the violent crime in our streets. A 1980 study by William Bowers and Glenn Pierce titled "Deterrence or Brutalization: What Is the Effect of Executions?" showed that the primary distinguishing characteristic between those imprisoned for homicide and those imprisoned for the lesser charge of aggravated assault was that the victims of the former were unarmed or intoxicated. Neither the killers' intent nor any deterrence by laws played a major part.

> At times, the deterrence myth bleeds over into outright lies or fantasy.

In fact, there is only one conceivable "deterrent" in the death penalty: that the person executed is undeniably prevented from committing a crime again. Yet if that narrow kind of "deterrence"—the irrevocable incapacitation of a single offender—is the only goal, incarceration, including, where appropriate, life without parole, provides as much protection for society.

Politicians Perpetuate the Myth

Yet politicians persist in trafficking in the deterrence myth. Some try to turn the failure of the death penalty to deter crime into a reason to pump up the capital-punishment machine even further: "If we're going to have a death penalty on the books, it ought to be a real deterrent," Connecticut's Governor John Rowland said in early 2001, arguing for speeding up executions and imposing the death penalty for more offenses.

At times, the deterrence myth bleeds over into outright lies or fantasy. In that October 2000 presidential debate, George W. Bush declared his capital-punishment apparatus in Texas part of a successful crime-fighting machine: "I'm proud of the fact that violent crime is down in the state of Texas. I'm proud of the fact that we hold people accountable."

Bush's crime-fighting success, unfortunately, is a figment of his imagination. According to figures in the FBI's Uniform Crime Reports released in the same month as the Bush-Gore debate, while crime is declining in cities nationwide, it is rising in the large cities of Texas. The FBI's figures confirm a study by the Justice Police Institute of Washington, D.C., which found crime falling more slowly in Bush's Texas than in any comparable state. The only other state to defy the national crime drop is Florida, which is also the only state to rival Texas in the pace of executions. By comparison New York, which although it has reinstated the death penalty has not actually executed anyone in decades, leads the nation's most populous states in driving crime downward.

Why, then, does the deterrence myth persist? Police know the death penalty doesn't deter crime. Crime-policy experts know it. The scholars know it. It is only politicians, it seems, who have not heard the news.

3

An Effective Death Penalty Protects the Community from Criminals

Kent Scheidegger

Kent Scheidegger is the legal director and general counsel of the Criminal Justice Legal Foundation, a nonprofit public interest law organization that aims to restore a balance between the rights of crime victims and the criminally accused.

State government has an obligation to keep its citizens safe from murderers. Recent studies indicate that the death penalty deters murder, and the five states showing the most improvement in their homicide rates actively use capital punishment. The death penalty in New Jersey is not effective because the state's Supreme Court justices are hostile to capital punishment and block its enforcement.

I thank the commission for the opportunity to testify today. The correct identification and sufficient punishment of murderers is a matter of the greatest importance. Indeed, there is no more important function of the state government than the protection of their citizens from murder. Regrettably, that function is not being properly performed in New Jersey today.

Saving Lives

In recent years, we have seen a sea change in the scholarship on deterrence and the death penalty. The availability of data for the 30 years since the restoration of capital punishment as

Kent Scheidegger, "Statement before the New Jersey Death Penalty Study Commission," www.cjlf.org, October 24, 2006, pp. 1–3. Reproduced by permission of the author.

well as improved methods of econometrics have produced a new generation of studies. While the studies are not unanimous and absolute proof is not possible, a preponderance of studies published in peer-reviewed journals confirms what common sense has always told us. The death penalty does have a deterrent effect and does save innocent lives *if* it is actually enforced.

I will not attempt to explain the math behind these studies or pretend that I completely understand it myself. To illustrate deterrence in more understandable terms, I have computed the change in the murder rate for each state using as a base the moratorium period from 1968 to 1975 when there were no executions in the United States and it was doubtful there ever would be any again. This gives us a basis to compare states at a time when none of them had an effective death penalty and see how they changed when the death penalty was restored. In 2004, the State of Delaware had the greatest drop since the moratorium period of any state in the nation, and Delaware has also had the most effective death penalty of any state by a wide margin. I do not believe this is a coincidence. Of the five states with the best improvements in their homicide rates, all five are states actively using the death penalty. Over 11,000 people were murdered in New Jersey between 1977 and 2004, and I believe it is probable that some of them would be alive today if the state had an effective death penalty during this time.

So why doesn't New Jersey have an effective death penalty? Thirty years of experience in 38 states has demonstrated one truth beyond question. You cannot have an effective death penalty in a state if your court of last resort is determined to block it and willing to twist the law to do so. Regrettably, that appears to be the case in New Jersey.

An Outrage

To see this, one need only look at the decision last July [2006] in the case of Anthony DiFrisco. DiFrisco was a hired killer, a hit man, who committed murder in 1986. In 1994, the New Jersey Supreme Court reviewed all his claims of procedural error and decided by a majority vote that no reversible error had occurred in his case. The next year, the court reviewed his claim that his sentence was disproportionate and decided 5-2 that it was not. Eleven years after that second decision and 20 years after the crime, the New Jersey Supreme Court went back, counted noses in its two previous decisions, decided it could put together a majority for reversal in those two decisions, and on that basis alone overturned the death sentence. Not only was the decision on the merits an outrage, but to reopen this eleven-year-old case, the court had to brush aside and effectively nullify a rule of court placing a five-year limit on collateral review of final judgments. After 20 years of litigating these matters, I thought I had seen it all. But this is beyond belief. This is not law in any meaningful sense of the word. This is pure obstruction of the enforcement of the law simply because a majority of the judges disagree with it, and they are willing to make up new rules without limit to impose their preference on the state.

Nor is the *DiFrisco* case the only outrage by any means. Earlier, you heard the poignant testimony of Sandra Place. Her elderly mother was strangled by a man who broke into her house and who then cut off her clothing and sexually violated her. The New Jersey Supreme Court held that the death penalty for this offense was disproportionate and struck it down. To reach this bizarre result, the court decided that for any disputed fact not conclusively resolved by the jury's verdict, it would presume that the defendant's version was the truth. This is diametrically opposed to the long-standing and universal rule of appellate practice throughout the United States. In reviewing jury verdicts, U.S. courts have uniformly assumed the version of the facts most favorable to the verdict. Nothing but pure hostility to the death penalty and a desire to block its enforcement can explain the gratuitous and unprecedented adoption of the opposite presumption.

31

The primary question before this commission and the Legislature and people of New Jersey is whether you are going to value the lives of the innocent above the lives of the guilty and do what it takes to actually have an effective death penalty in this state. Several measures suggest themselves.

The execution of a person who is in fact guilty of murder and is in fact eligible for the death penalty is not an injustice warranting multiple reviews over a period of 20 years.

Supreme Court at Fault

First, get rid of proportionality review. It is not constitutionally required, and it is not needed as a practical matter. The criteria to be eligible for the death penalty, the jury's decision informed by every mitigating fact the defendant chooses to offer, and the final backstop of executive clemency make this additional level of review unnecessary. The New Jersey Supreme Court wastes resources trying to quantify a fundamentally unquantifiable decision, and the case of the murder of Mildred Place demonstrates that the court cannot be trusted to do this correctly.

Second, enact some strong limits on collateral review. Every capital defendant should be entitled to a direct appeal and one post-conviction proceeding, and there should be no further reviews of any issue that does not raise a substantial doubt of the identity of the perpetrator. The execution of a person who is in fact guilty of murder and is in fact eligible for the death penalty is not an injustice warranting multiple reviews over a period of 20 years.

Finally, though, nothing will achieve the goal unless you fix the New Jersey Supreme Court. We hear a lot about judicial independence. But the other, equally important side of that coin is judicial responsibility. Judges must use their power for its proper purpose of enforcing the Constitution and not for the improper purpose of imposing their policy preferences on the people of the state. Unfortunately, life tenure tempts too many judges to do exactly that. I suggest that New Jersey amend its Constitution so that Justices of the Supreme Court must go before the people for a yes or no confirmation at regular intervals, as is done in California. The experience in California demonstrates that this system comes as close as possible to the optimum, providing effective life tenure in most cases while still providing a safety valve to remove the most egregious abusers of judicial power.

4

The Death Penalty Saves Lives

William Otis

William Otis is the counselor to the head of the Drug Enforcement Administration, U.S. Department of Justice.

Death penalty abolitionists do not take into account the brutality or cold-bloodedness of some murders, such as murders-for-hire. The punishment should fit the crime. During the ten-year moratorium period (1967–1977), in which no executions took place in the United States, the number of murders doubled from the previous ten-year period, during which 289 executions took place. The death penalty saves lives.

I want to start off by telling you a story about something that happened in . . . Silver Spring, Maryland. A family lived there by the name of Horn. They had a little boy by the name of Trevor. Trevor had a difficult birth. There was a botched delivery. The umbilical cord became wrapped around his neck and he was deprived of oxygen for a significant period of time during the delivery. He was born a quadriplegic with significant mental retardation. As a result of this, he got a $1.7 million settlement from the hospital.

Raising a quadriplegic son is a difficult enterprise, and it's expensive even when you have a big settlement. When Trevor was eight years old, his father Lawrence Horn had had enough of these difficulties and decided that this big pile of money that had been put aside for his son could be put to a better

William Otis, "The Death Penalty Today: Defend It, Mend It or End It?" *The Pew Forum on Religion & Public Life*, July 21, 2006, pp. 10–12. Copyright © 2000–2007 *The Pew Forum on Religion & Public Life*. Reproduced by permission of the author.

usc; namcly, his use. So he arranged to have Trevor killed. This is not something he did by himself; he hired a hit man.

Strictly Business

You might think I'm making up that someone would hire a hit man to kill an eight-year-old, but it's true. The hit man's name was James Perry. There was a considerable amount of price haggling about how much Lawrence Horn would pay to have his kid killed. Some of that price haggling was done over the phone; some of it was done with an intermediary who testified at the trial. The parts that were done over the phone amazingly enough were left on phone answering machine messages. And those were introduced along with other telephone records at the trial.

The reason a hit man shoots his victims through the eyes is so that in the unlikely event the victim survives, he or she will not be able to do an in-court identification.

Eventually, a price was agrccd upon—$5,000—but included in this, Lawrcncc Horn wanted not merely his son to be killed; he also wanted his wife to be killed because, you see, his wife would've shared in the $1.7 million, and he wanted it all for himself. So the deal was $5,000 to kill the eight-year-old and kill the eight-year-old's mother.

James Perry went out to the house and he made good on the contract. Killing an eight-year-old, particularly a paralyzed one, is not very difficult for an adult male who just put his hand over the tube that fed oxygen into Trevor's trachea. But killing the mother involved a little more than that and indeed there was a complication. The complication was that Trevor's nurse was also there. Her name was Janice Saunders. So James Perry was confronted with an unexpected and unwanted witness to this. He shot the mother and he also shot Janice Saunders, thc nurse. He shot them through the eyes. Now you might think that this just shows what a gruesome, horrible, sadistic person this guy was, but that's not so. The reason a hit man shoots his victims through the eyes is so that in the unlikely event the victim survives, he or she will not be able to do an in-court identification. It wasn't sadism, it wasn't a mental defect, it was just business.

The burden of proof in this debate about the death penalty is on the abolitionist side, and it is not merely to show that there are questionable or sympathetic or problematic cases, as there are in every aspect of litigation. What they must show is that every execution is wrong. Abolition means abolition, the end of it—period.

Flaws in the Abolitionist Argument

There are two central problems, I think, with a strict abolitionist argument. One is that it is a one-size-fits-all, don't-pester-me-with-the-facts sort of position. It simply does not matter, under that position, what the killer did, how utterly incontestable the evidence is of his guilt, how gruesome or cold blooded or calculated it was, how many people he killed, or how many people he killed in the past. None of that matters. A position like that significantly oversteps the justifications typically offered on behalf of the abolitionist position: bad lawyering, possible racism in any given case, that the police are hiding or manufacturing evidence. All of those things can be gone over and are gone over in great detail and over a long period of review in case-by-case analysis under the most exacting standards that the law knows. But that is a far cry from justifying complete abolition in every case no matter what.

Let the punishment fit the crime.

Indeed, an argument that the death penalty should be abolished, period, no matter what the circumstances, deliberately ignoring the circumstances, is an argument that in most neutral settings—including, for example, court and sensible law school debates—would not be taken seriously. The public does not take it seriously. Support for the death penalty in this country is at 65 percent; it has been at about that same level for a number of years now. A Gallup poll [in June 2006] . . . pointed out that a majority of the country believes that the death penalty is not imposed frequently enough. There is probably not one single abolitionist on the current Supreme Court. In the history of the court, there have been 112 justices; three of them—Brennan, Marshall, and Blackmun—have been against the death penalty per se. The other 109 have not.

Appropriate Punishment?

The second basic, overriding problem with outright abolitionism is that it simply shoves off to one side what in any other context is the accepted and indeed the uncontroversial maxim that governs criminal punishment, and that is that the punishment should fit the crime. What punishment do you think fits the crime that James Perry and Lawrence Horn committed? A sentence of imprisonment no matter what the length? It's fine to give a long sentence to a carjacker, to a child molester, to someone who poisons kids—teenagers by selling them dangerous drugs, for instance—but that is a different kind of thing. It's frequently said in these debates that death is different. It is different and so are the crimes like Lawrence Horn's and James Perry's and Timothy McVeigh's that bring about the death penalty. Let the punishment fit the crime.

I would be hard pressed to tell you that there is anything in the law that could not benefit from reformation, but I think what we need to watch out for is abolition being impersonated by a call for reformation. And in particular I want to mention the call for a death penalty moratorium, which in my opinion is abolition in disguise. Death penalty opponents know that they cannot sell outright abolition because the public is against it. The public has seen enough of Timothy McVeigh and John Wayne Gacy and some of these other gruesome killers and is simply unwilling to put aside for all time and in any circumstances its right to allow the jury to decide on a death penalty. So we hear the call for a moratorium.

Proof of Deterrent Effect

And the last thought I want to leave you with . . . is this: we have had a moratorium before in this country. It lasted for ten years, from 1967 to 1977. In the preceding ten years when we had executions—289 of them—there were 95,000 murders in this country. Immediately after that, during the 10-year moratorium from 1967 to 1977, we of course had zero executions and 180,000 murders—almost double the number. The truth of the matter is that the death penalty has a significant deterrent effect as these numbers prove beyond serious argument. Therefore it is the death penalty and not abolition of the death penalty that in the end will save innocent life.

5

The Death Penalty Keeps Americans Safe from Terrorist Threats

George W. Bush

George W. Bush is the forty-third president of the United States.

After the terrorist attacks of September 11, 2001, it became apparent that the best strategy for the war on terror is to stay on the offensive against terrorists. In order to protect and defend America more effectively, the Department of Homeland Security was created and the Patriot Act was signed into law. Law enforcement and intelligence agencies are now able to share information about terrorist threats. The Patriot Act's anti-terrorism provisions are set to expire, and Congress must renew them in order to keep Americans safe. Congress should also change the law so that all terrorist-related crimes resulting in death will qualify for capital punishment. Our country needs to use all available crime-fighting tools, including the death penalty, to send a strong message to terrorists and to protect America.

I want to thank the community leaders who are here from around the great Commonwealth of Pennsylvania. I appreciate your service to our country. . . . We share a common calling, and that's public service, serving our nation. . . . You and I know what our first responsibility is; the first responsibility, whether it be Washington, D.C. or Washington Township, is the safety of our citizens. That's a solemn duty we have, to work together to make sure that our nation is as secure as it can possibly be.

George W. Bush, "President Bush Calls for Renewing the USA PATRIOT Act," www .whitehouse.gov, April 19, 2004.

The task, our mutual tasks, our joint obligation changed dramatically on September the 11th, 2001. There's now an urgency to our duty. We have a urgent duty to do everything we can to fulfill our solemn obligation.

There are people here in this world who still want to hurt us. See, they can't stand America. They can't stand us because we love certain things and we're not going to change. We love our freedom. We love the fact that we can worship freely any way we see fit. We love the fact that we can speak our minds freely. We love our free political process. We love every aspect of freedom and we refuse to change. These terrorists will not be stopped by their own conscience; they don't have a conscience. But they will be stopped. They will be stopped because our great nation is resolute abroad, we're vigilant at home, and we are absolutely determined to prevail. . . .

The War on Terror

As we gather this afternoon, we're 140 miles away from Shanksville, Pennsylvania. This is a place where many innocent lives ended. Shanksville is also the place where American citizens stood up to evil, charged their attackers and began the first counter-offensive in the war on terror. Those passengers on Flight 93 showed that the spirit of America is strong and brave in the face of danger. And this nation will always honor their memory.

The best way to secure our homeland, the best way for us to do our duty, is to stay on the offensive against the terrorist network. We began the offense shortly after September the 11th. We're carrying out a broad strategy, a worldwide strategy to bring the killers to justice. The best way to secure America is to bring them to justice before they hurt us again, which is precisely what the United States of America will continue to do.

Two-thirds of known al Qaeda leaders have been captured or killed. We're making progress. It's a different kind of war than the war that Major [Dick] Winters [a World War II veteran] fought in. This is a war against people who will hide in a cave; a war against people who hide in the shadows of remote cities, or big cities, and then they strike and they kill. And they kill innocent people. They have no—as I said, they have no conscience, they have no sense of guilt. But they also know we're on their trail. And they will find out there is no cave or hole deep enough to hide from American justice.

We're not going to forget September the 11th.

We must be determined in this, and we've got a lot of really good people, a lot of good people on the move. We're also working with nations from around the world, sharing intelligence, making it clear that if you harbor a terrorist, you're just as guilty as the terrorist. . . .

The enemy is still active. Think about [the terrorist bombing in October 2002 in] Bali and [the terrorist bombings in November 2003 in] Istanbul, or as we saw in the murder of 200 citizens in Madrid [on March 11, 2004]. The terrorists use violence to spread fear and disrupt elections. They want us to panic. That's their intent. Their intent is to say, let's create panic among the civilized world. They want nations to turn upon each other, civilized nations to argue and debate about the mission. You know, they're not going to shake our will. I'll say as plainly as I can to them: You'll never shake the will of the United States of America. We're not going to forget September the 11th. We are determined, we are resolute, and we will bring you to justice.

A New Line of Defense

And in the process, we've made some fundamental changes in the way we defend ourself. We reorganized—or organized a new Department of Homeland Security to protect the country. It was hard work in the Senate. . . . We had a big debate about it, but it was the right thing to do. It was the right thing to bring agencies involved with the protection of the homeland under one umbrella agency, so we can better coordinate and better communicate and better strategize as to how to protect the homeland. . . .

The FBI now has the prevention of terrorist attacks as their number one priority. They'll still chase down criminals and make a case. But since we're at war, and since this is a big, free country, the priority of the federal government is now the prevention of another attack. And we're making sure they got the resources necessary to do their job.

We're standing behind our first responders. Since the moment our country was attacked, our nation's police and firefighters and emergency service personnel have played a critical role in the defense of America against any threat of terror. They really have. It was a—we saw the incredible bravery of the first responders in New York City. I think it—I think those who are firefighters and police and emergency personnel gained a new degree of respect on the streets of the cities throughout our country, when they witnessed the great courage of their brothers who rushed into collapsing buildings. We appreciate the fact that these men and women understand they'll be on the front line against terror at any moment, that they have accepted great responsibilities. . . .

The Patriot Act

After September the 11th, we took another vital step to fight terror, and that's what I want to talk about today. I want to talk about the Patriot Act. It's a law that I signed into law. It's a law that was overwhelmingly passed in the House and the Senate. It's a law that is making America safer. It's an important piece of legislation.

First, before September the 11th, law enforcement, intelligence, and national security officials were prevented by legal and bureaucratic restrictions from sharing critical information with each other, and with state and local police departments.

We had—one group of the FBI knows something, but they couldn't talk to the other group in the FBI—because of law and bureaucratic interpretation. You cannot fight the war on terror unless all bodies of your government at the federal, state, and local level are capable of sharing intelligence on a real-time basis. We could not get a complete picture of terrorist threats, therefore. People had—different people had a piece of the puzzle, but because of law, they couldn't get all the pieces in the same place. And so we removed those barriers, removed the walls. You hear the talk about the walls that separate certain aspects of government; they have been removed by the Patriot Act. And now, law enforcement and intelligence communities are working together to share information to better prevent an attack on America. . . .

Before September the 11th, federal judges could often impose tougher prison terms on drag traffickers than they could on terrorists.

[In late 2001] police in Portland, Oregon turned up evidence about a local man who was planning attacks on Jewish schools and synagogues, and on American troops overseas. The initial information was passed to the FBI and to intelligence services—quickly passed—who analyzed the threat and took action. See, the Patriot Act allowed for unprecedented cooperation. And because of the surveillance tools enacted by the Patriot Act, the FBI learned that this guy was a part of a seven-man terrorist cell. In other words, the Patriot Act gave local—federal law enforcement officials, in this case—the capacity to better understand the intelligence and to better understand the nature of the terrorist cell. And now the cell has been disrupted. . . .

Sending a Strong Signal

Before September the 11th, federal judges could often impose tougher prison terms on drug traffickers than they could on terrorists. The Patriot Act strengthened the penalties for crimes committed by terrorists, such as arsons, or attacks on power plants and mass transit systems. In other words, we needed to get—we needed to send the signal, at the very minimum, that our laws are going to be tough on you. When we catch you, you've got a problem, in America. See, that's part of prevention. . . .

I want you to keep in mind what I've just told you about the Patriot Act the next time you hear somebody attacking the Patriot Act. The Patriot Act defends our liberty. The Patriot Act makes it able for those of us in positions of responsibility to defend the liberty of the American people. It's essential law.

We ought to be sending a strong signal: If you sabotage a defense installation or nuclear facility in a way that takes an innocent life, you ought to get the death penalty.

The reason I bring it up is because many of the Patriot Act's anti-terrorism tools are set to expire next year [in 2005], including key provisions that allow our intelligence and law enforcement agencies to share information. In other words, Congress passed it and said, well, maybe the war on terror won't go on very long, and, therefore, these tools are set to expire. The problem is, the war on terror continues. And yet some senators and congressmen not only want to let the provisions expire, but they want to roll back some of the act's permanent features. And it doesn't make any sense. We can't return to the days of false hope. The terrorists declared war on the United States of America. And the Congress must give law enforcement all the tools necessary to protect the American people.

So I'm starting today to call on the United States Congress to renew the Patriot Act and to make all of its provisions permanent. And not only that, there are some additional things that Congress should do—must do, in my judgment—to strengthen authorities and penalties to defend our homeland. . . .

People charged with certain crimes today, including some drug offenses, are eligible for bail only in limited circumstances. But terrorist-related crimes are not on that list. Think about what that means. Suspected terrorists could be released, free to leave the country, or worse, before their trial. And that doesn't make any sense. The disparity makes no sense. If a dangerous drug dealer can be held without bail, the Congress should allow the same treatment for terrorists. If we want to protect our homeland, let's make sure these good people have got the tools necessary to do so.

And there's another example I want to share with you. Under existing law, the death penalty applies to many serious crimes that result in death, including sexual abuse and certain drug-related offenses. Some terrorist crimes that result in death do not qualify for capital punishment. That makes no sense to me. We ought to be sending a strong signal: If you sabotage a defense installation or nuclear facility in a way that takes an innocent life, you ought to get the death penalty, the federal death penalty.

Protecting America

The reason why Congress must act is because we have a difficult job protecting America. The reason why is because we're an open society that values freedom. We stand for the—we're a beacon of freedom and we say you can—our country is an open country. And yet that makes us vulnerable—in itself, makes us vulnerable. We got a lot of borders to protect. We got to be right a hundred percent of the time, at the federal level and the state level and the local level. We've got to be right a hundred percent of the time to protect America, and the terrorists have only got to be right one time—as 168 innocent men, women and children found out in Oklahoma City [in the bombing of the federal building on April 19, 1995]. Different forms of terror. We've got to be vigilant against terror at all costs.

And there's only one path to safety and that's the path of action. Congress must act with the Patriot Act. We must continue to stay on the offense when it comes to chasing these killers down and bringing them to justice—and we will. We've got to be strong and resolute and determined. We will never show weakness in the face of these people who have no soul, who have no conscience, who care less about the life of a man or a woman or a child. We've got to do everything we can here at home. And there's no doubt in my mind that, with the Almighty's blessings and hard work, that we will succeed in our mission.

6

The Death Penalty Hinders the Fight Against Terrorism

American Civil Liberties Union

The American Civil Liberties Union is a nonprofit organization that works in courts, legislatures, and communities to defend and preserve the individual rights and freedoms guaranteed by the U.S. Constitution. The ACLU's Capital Punishment Project challenges the unfairness and arbitrariness of capital punishment while working toward its ultimate repeal.

The death penalty tarnishes the international image of the United States as a moral leader. International media, particularly in Europe, provide coverage of U.S. executions and capital punishment issues in a critical and derogatory manner. The death penalty hinders cooperation in the war on terror, because allies opposing capital punishment may refuse to extradite alleged terrorists to countries in which the death penalty is a possibility.

> *It is important for the United States to maintain [its international image] in the eyes of Europeans, and to protect the legitimacy of our moral leadership. This moral leadership is under challenge because of two issues: the death penalty and violence in our society.*
>
> *Felix G. Rohatyn,*
> *U.S. ambassador to France from 1997 to 2000.*

American Civil Liberties Union, *How the Death Penalty Weakens U.S. International Interests*. Durham, NC: ACLU Capital Punishment Project, 2004. Copyright © 2004 ACLU. Reproduced by permission.

While the death penalty is receiving increased attention in the United States, media coverage in Europe of U.S. executions typically is both more extensive and more critical than domestic coverage. Executions that go relatively unnoticed in the United States often make headlines in Europe, drawing criticism from conservative and liberal publications alike. U.S. executions evoke much passion in Europe, and often spark protests in front of our embassies, as well as petitions calling for an end to executions.

International Image in the Press

One important and generally conservative publication that has been particularly outspoken regarding the U.S. death penalty is the British magazine, The *Economist*. The magazine, which is read widely by business people in Europe, the United States, and around the world, is known for promoting business-friendly public policies and tax reductions, and it endorsed George W. Bush in his first presidential election. The *Economist* also, however, has made clear its opposition to the death penalty in the United States.

The *Economist* has called the United States "the most glaring exception to the emerging international consensus on the death penalty." Noting that the United States defends the practice to its allies and continues to execute juvenile offenders and the mentally retarded, the magazine asked, "Why is the world's richest, and arguably greatest democracy, so out of step?" Another opinion piece in The *Economist* calling for the abolition of the death penalty in the United States noted that even the United States, with its legal guarantees and complex system of appeals, is unable to ensure the fair or consistent application of the death penalty. The *Economist* concluded that the inevitable execution of innocents is too high a price to pay for an unnecessary punishment.

These clear statements of The *Economist*'s opposition to the death penalty are in addition to numerous news articles criticizing the execution of the mentally retarded, flaws relating to legal representation and the appellate process in death penalty cases, and errors in the application of the death penalty. This is the image of the United States portrayed to sophisticated business people worldwide by a leading and generally conservative international publication.

Other international media outlets also provide regular and extensive coverage of U.S. death penalty issues as well as of individual executions. The coverage often is critical of the death penalty, and such criticism comes from conservative as well as liberal publications. This has been an important factor in shaping the international image of the United States. One example is the coverage by the *Sun*, one of Britain's most conservative newspapers, of a ... [February 2000] elementary school shooting in Michigan. When a 6-year-old shot and killed a classmate, the *Sun* editorialized that the most likely American response would be to build a kiddie-size electric chair.

Allies Criticize Executions

Because of the notoriously large number of executions in Texas, the election of former Texas governor George W. Bush as president has inspired even broader foreign coverage of the U.S. death penalty. One Swiss newspaper, for example, marked President Bush's inauguration by printing all the photographs it could find of prisoners in Texas who had been executed on his watch. The *Mirror*, a popular British newspaper, printed a six-page story on President Bush titled, "The Texas Massacre." The article stated: "Bush makes no apology for his hideous track record. And disturbingly, he has mass support from Americans, driven by their out-of-control gun culture and blood lust for retribution."

As a result of the extensive media coverage of the death penalty, Europeans' image of President Bush, as well as of the United States, is greatly affected by the death penalty. As stated by Claudia Roth, a member of the German parliament: "What we know about the new president, is just two things. He is the son of President Bush, and he has sent 150 people to their death in Texas, including the mentally ill."

The case of Timothy McVeigh, the first federal execution in 38 years [on June 11, 2001], attracted widespread media attention, particularly following revelations that authorities failed to give thousands of relevant documents to McVeigh's lawyers before his trial. A *Time* columnist stated that development "added a baffling and embarrassing new example to the dozens of instances of judicial error, mendacious testimony, incompetent defense lawyers and sloppy lab work that have demonstrably sent innocent people to their deaths in recent years."

This episode, together with the viewing of the execution by two dozen live witnesses and another 300 over closed-circuit television, led to intense public scrutiny of the case, both in the United States and abroad. Press coverage in Europe and other regions was both extensive and derogatory towards the United States. The Council of Europe labeled the execution "sad, pathetic and wrong." Amnesty International called it, "a failure of human rights leadership at the highest level of government in the United States"

Seeking the death penalty for terrorists could ultimately work against the process of international teamwork that has led to several successful convictions.

Even before the attention generated by the McVeigh case, the death penalty affected the international interests of the United States. Felix Rohatyn, former U.S. ambassador to France, wrote in the *Washington Post* about the challenge to America's moral leadership in Europe over the death penalty. He said that during his time in France, no single issue evoked as much passion and protest. Ambassador Rohatyn noted that the U.S. ambassador to Germany encountered challenges on the issue just as frequently. He concluded that, "At a time when our military, economic, and political power, our so-called 'hegemony,' is a source of concern to many of our allies, it is important that our moral leadership be sustained."

Cooperation in the "War on Terror"

International opposition to the death penalty also may be hindering U.S. efforts against international terrorism. As former CIA official Michael Bearden argued in the *Wall Street Journal*, seeking the death penalty for terrorists could ultimately work against the process of international teamwork that has led to several successful convictions in this area. Countries such as Pakistan, Kenya, and South Africa have delivered accused terrorists to U.S. courts without formal extradition processes. Bearden believes that seeking the death penalty in such cases could complicate or limit such cooperation in the future.

In May 2004, the direct impact of the United States' policy became clearly visible. Muslim cleric Abu Hamza was arrested in Great Britain on a U.S. warrant, which included allegations of 11 separate charges of terrorism and terrorist activity. However, British law forbids the Home Secretary from extraditing someone to a country where the death penalty applies for the offense charged, unless there has been a written agreement not to carry out the sentence of death should it be imposed. U.S. Attorney General John Ashcroft had to come to an explicit agreement with Great Britain not to execute Abu Hamza if Ashcroft wanted Hamza extradited to face a trial in U.S. courts.

The problems caused by the death penalty issue, and the close attention paid to it abroad, likely will not subside. While over 930 prisoners have been executed in the United States since 1976, another 3,500 are currently on death row [as of 2004]. Meanwhile, the number of crimes for which the death penalty is available has increased since its reinstatement by the

U.S. Supreme Court [in 1976]. As executions continue in the United States, so too will the damage to its international image and moral leadership.

7

The Death Penalty Encourages Terrorism

Thomas McDonnell

Thomas McDonnell is a professor at Pace University School of Law in White Plains, New York.

Convicted for his role in the September 11, 2001, terrorist attacks against the United States, Zacarias Moussaoui wished to be put to death but instead was sentenced to life imprisonment. Many terrorists are not deterred by the death penalty because they do not fear death, as evidenced by their willingness to take part in suicide bombing plots. U.S.-imposed capital punishment may actually encourage terrorists, who believe they will become martyrs if executed.

A federal jury from the conservative Eastern District of Virginia has denied Zacarias Moussaoui his apparent wish—to become a martyr at the hands of the United States. The only person convicted in the United States of Sept. 11, 2001-related crimes and sometimes called the Barney Fife [character created by Don Knotts on *The Andy Griffith Show*] of al-Qaeda, Moussaoui seems to have done all he could have in the sentencing trial to guarantee a trip to the death chamber.

Deserving of Death

Contradicting his previous accounts, Moussaoui testified in the first part of the trial against the advice of his lawyers, claiming for the first time that he and failed shoe bomber Ri-

Thomas McDonnell, "Death Penalty Won't Deter Terrorism," *New Jersey Law Journal*, June 5, 2006. Copyright © 2006. 2006 ALM Properties, Inc. This article is reprinted with permission from *New Jersey Law Journal*.

chard Reid were to fly a plane into the White House on 9/11 and that he lied to FBI agents upon his arrest, precisely what the government had been arguing to justify a death sentence. (Moussaoui, himself, had been in jail for 26 days on 9/11.) During the second part of the trial, Moussaoui openly and repeatedly mocked the families of the 9/11 victims, saying he regretted that more Americans had not been killed.

Four days after Moussaoui was sentenced to life without possibility of parole, after the jury could not unanimously agree on a death sentence, he moved to withdraw his guilty plea. He now claims that he lied at trial about his involvement in 9/11. U.S. District Court Judge Leonie Brinkema summarily denied his motion.

Moussaoui's strange case invites an examination of whether we should impose capital punishment on those involved in acts of terrorism against the United States, its institutions and its people. If anyone deserves the death penalty, then those who planned and actively participated in the 9/11 conspiracy do. The United States will almost certainly execute such participants, including Mohammed Shaikh Khalid, Ramzi bin al-Shibh and Abu Zubaydah, assuming that it chooses to try them and they are found responsible, as expected, for the 9/11 attacks.

Encouraging Terrorism

Yet after more than four years in the "war on terrorism" have passed, a grudging recognition is beginning to arise that we need the United Nations, the help of our allies and respect for the rule of law. Similarly, the natural demand for retribution after a terrorist organization has committed mass murder and other heinous crimes needs to be tempered by the fact that carrying out the death penalty may strengthen the terrorists.

Because 19 hijackers were willing to kill themselves to carry out the 9/11 crimes and because al-Qaeda and its related organizations continue to use suicide bombers, the threat of the death penalty is not likely to deter similar actors in the future. In fact, in a perverse way, the death penalty might actually encourage such actors. If caught, they can still be martyrs after being executed by the U.S. government.

Given the perceived and actual grievances that the Arab and Islamic worlds have toward the West in general and the United States in particular, carrying out such executions may tend to inflame the Arab and Islamic worlds, increase their support of terrorist movements and thwart cooperation with our allies, almost all of whom have abolished the death penalty. U.S. attorneys can argue, however, that even if suicide bombers may not be generally deterred, and even if executing terrorists causes some repercussions, those with any responsibility for the 9/11 attacks, the worst crimes ever committed on American soil, warrant the death penalty.

As [renowned English jurist] Lord Justice [Alfred Thompson] Denning stated, "The truth is that some crimes are so outrageous that society insists on adequate punishment, because the wrong-doer deserves it, irrespective of whether it is a deterrent or not."

Contradictions

Yale law professor Charles Black observed, however, that the death penalty is an evil, because, among other things, "it extinguishes, after untellable suffering, the most mysterious and wonderful thing we know, human life; this reason has many harmonics." Such harmonics may include strengthening support in the Arab and Muslim world for al-Qaeda and its related groups and disciples. So instead of clinging to capital punishment, we will probably do better by turning off the klieg lights [powerful lamps used in making movies] of the death penalty theater.

Despite the jury's conclusion in its somewhat contradictory special verdict that the defense had failed to establish Moussaoui's potential martydom as a mitigating factor,

Brinkema in sentencing him, told Moussaoui what rejecting the death penalty signified: "You came here to be a martyr and to die in a big bang of glory, but, to paraphrase the poet T.S. Eliot, you will die with a whimper."

8

Capital Punishment Maintains Law and Order

Mufti Zubair Bayat

Mufti Zubair Bayat is the founder and as of 1999 was the director of the Darul Ihsan Research and Education Centre (DIRECT) in South Africa, a nonprofit institute committed to serving the cause of Islam and Muslims on a global level through education, research, and publications. He is also the media officer of Jamiat-KZN and serves as editor of the Al-Jamiat *newspaper.*

Crime, particularly murder, has become rampant since the abolition of the death penalty in South Africa. The judicial system is not meting out appropriate punishment to dangerous criminals, whose shorter prison sentences allow them to continue preying on law-abiding citizens. By killing others, murderers have forfeited their own right to life. Countries with capital punishment have lower crime rates, proving the deterrent effect of executions. South Africa should reinstate the death penalty to restore law and order.

The abolition of the death sentence along with the [South African] government's playing deaf to the pleas of ordinary crime-ridden, fear-stricken citizens of the country on this matter, has only exacerbated the already intolerable murder rate. There is no more deterring factor left for cold-blooded, callous murderers, who have become totally brazen in taking the lives of innocent men, women and children for trivial material gain and at times for nothing at all.

Mufti Zubair Bayat, "Capital Punishment: A Deterrent to Serious Crime," *Jamiatul Ulama (KwaZulu-Natal)*, June 7, 1999. Reproduced by permission of the author.

On the other hand, the sweeping amnesties granted by the state to hardened criminals and releasing them almost within months after having committed heinous crimes against the law-abiding citizens of the country on the flimsy grounds of over-crowding prisons, has not helped the situation in any way. It is quite common these days, to hear of dangerous prisoners being released after having spent only a fraction of their long sentences behind bars. Many others have escaped and are at large, carrying on a crime-riddled existence with total impunity.

Murderers' Right to Life Forfeited

Much support is ostensibly taken by the judiciary for the repealing of the death sentence from the Bill of Rights that entrenches the right to life. This may be so, but did not the murdered person have the right to his or her life in the first instance? Has not the murderer forfeited his own right to life by taking the life of another? Yet the murderer is virtually shielded and protected from severe retribution by the judicial establishment of this country, by its quaint verdicts to the extent that he is allowed to continue with his aggression against fellow beings within months of his previous convictions. Hardly any one seems to have the power to do anything about the situation, while criminals are enjoying a field day. This prevalent state of affairs is nothing short of blatant injustice.

If this country is to enjoy any degree of peace, stability and economic progress, crime would have to be stamped out vigorously. As much as the South African Police Services are trying to arrest criminals and bring them to book, they are fighting a hopeless battle as long as the judicial system in this country is not drastically revised. Appropriate punishment of criminals, that would serve as clear deterrents to other criminals, is essential to bring back some semblance of law and order to this trouble-torn land.

The ... tidal wave of crime pounding our society [in the late 1990s] has rendered human life extremely cheap and worthless. Human life has to be accorded the respect it deserves. Those individuals in society that do not show respect towards the lives of fellow beings, themselves do not deserve the sacred and precious gift of life. Murder is the antithesis of life. The murderer is an aggressor against the individual and society. Protecting the murderer by abolishing the death sentence is aggression against the society and mankind at large.

The Restoration of Law and Order

One serious danger of abolishing capital punishment is that it could well lead to retaliatory attacks by frustrated relatives and friends of the victim. This seeking of revenge and retaliation could further lead to faction fights and gang warfare and this would result in murder and mayhem of a far greater scale. This in turn could result in the total breakdown of law and order. If the family of the deceased have some kind of assurance that the offender against their beloved one would be dealt with within the confines of proper justice, it would not lead to the unnecessary loss of other lives. In fact, many lives would be protected in the process. Proper and appropriate justice in the instance of murder and other serious offences would mean retribution by capital punishment and not in a prison sentence that could be commuted at a later date to a lesser term in prison as is the current judicial trend.

In those countries of the world where capital punishment is still in operation, the crime rate, especially murder, is distinctively low in comparison to countries where capital punishment has been discarded.

It has been observed that in those countries of the world where capital punishment is still in operation, the crime rate, especially murder, is distinctively low in comparison to countries where capital punishment has been discarded. Notable in this regard is that in some of the Islamic countries in the Middle East where capital punishment is absolutely meted out to murderers and other serious offenders, the crime rate is virtually nil. Such fear has been instilled in the minds of would-be criminals by the firm action of law-enforcement agencies, that the rate and odd case of murder receives unprecedented coverage by the media and generates much concern in the general public. Recently, visitors from this country to some of those countries could hardly believe their eyes at the relative safety and security that prevails in those lands, even in the late hours of the night, whereas the ordinary citizen living in this country is living in constant fear and apprehension even in broad day light regarding the safety of his very life and property. Enhanced security and alarm systems are not the answer to the problem nor is an increase in police presence the solution. The solution to this problem is simply the re-ordaining of Capital Punishment and a completely fresh approach towards crime and criminal activities by the Judiciary of this country.

A loud and clear message has to be sent to all potential criminals and murderers in particular, that murder is the greatest crime, an open violation of the basic human right to life, hence the penalty of violating such a right has to be extreme, that being capital punishment. It is the only way of maintaining the harmonious existence of man on earth along with his fellow beings. No human being, no matter who he may be, has the right to deny another human being this basic right to justice.

Worthy of praise and commendation are those pressure groups that are working at grass roots level to campaign for the re-instatement of the death penalty. An appeal is directed to the majority of the law-abiding citizens of the country to lend this cause their full support in which ever way possible. Enough is enough!!

9

Modern Societies Do Not Deter Crime with Capital Punishment

Chris Patten

Chris Patten served as external relations commissioner for the European Union (EU) from 1999 to 2004, and in 2005 he took his seat in the House of Lords. Lord Patten's publications include Not Quite the Diplomat: Home Truths About World Affairs *(2005). The following speech was written by Patten, but it was actually presented to the First World Congress by Angel Viñas.*

The member states of the European Union concur that the death penalty is inhumane, does not deter crime, and should be abolished worldwide. Through programs that promote human rights and democracy, the EU attempts to heighten public awareness of the incongruity of capital punishment in modern, free societies. The EU also engages in dialogue with countries that still use the death penalty, such as China, Iran, and the United States, to address specific human rights issues related to the death penalty's application.

Some 50 years ago a movement started in Europe to abolish the death penalty. Since then, all of the EU [European Union] Member States have abandoned this punishment. This afternoon [June 21, 2001], the twentieth anniversary of France's abolition will be celebrated. Its abolition in 1981 was very much the result of a long battle fought by one man,

Chris Patten, "Speech for the First World Congress Against the Death Penalty, Intervention at the Council of Europe, delivered by Angel Vinas, on behalf of The Rt Hon Chris Patten," eurunion.org, June 21, 2001, pp. 1–3. Reproduced by permission of the author.

[French Minister of Justice] Mr. [Robert] Badinter. We are immensely grateful for all of your efforts, Mr. Badinter.

Although Member States' experience of abolition has differed, they have shared common ground: they insist on the inhumane, unnecessary and irreversible character of capital punishment, no matter how cruel the crime committed by the offender. Furthermore, this logic now seems to be shared by the international community as a whole, insofar as both the Rome Statute of the International Criminal Court and the United Nations Security Council Resolutions establishing the International Criminal Tribunals for the former Yugoslavia and for Rwanda do not provide for the death penalty among the range of sanctions, even when the most serious crimes, including genocide, crimes against humanity and war crimes are tried.

The Inherent Dignity of All Human Beings

The EU has decided, as an integral part of its human rights policy, to strengthen its international activities in opposition to the death penalty. The EU is opposed to the death penalty in all circumstances and has agreed to campaign for its universal abolition. That stance is rooted in our belief in the inherent dignity of all human beings and the inviolability of the human person. This EU commitment was also reaffirmed in the EU Charter on Fundamental Rights, which was officially proclaimed at the Nice Summit in December 2000.

The EU believes that it is impossible to reduce to zero the risk of applying the penalty in error. That risk alone, the risk of taking innocent life, is reason enough for many of us to outlaw it as a punishment. Nor do we accept the argument that the death penalty is a deterrent to violent crime. In our countries the evidence simply does not support that claim.

The EU therefore works towards the universal abolition of the death penalty. In the process of attaining this objective, where the death penalty still exists, the EU calls for its use to be progressively restricted, and insists that it be carried out according to minimum standards. The EU also presses, where relevant, for moratoria to be introduced. The EU has produced internal guidelines for the demarches and representations it makes on capital punishment, where relevant, in multilateral fora and towards third countries.

Abolition is also a requirement for countries seeking EU membership. Almost all of the candidate countries have acceded to Protocol No. 6 to the European Convention on Human Rights concerning the Abolition of the Death Penalty. There is only one exception: Turkey.

We also actively pursue this policy in international human rights fora. A recent example is the EU initiative at the UN-Commission for Human Rights [CHR] in Geneva last April [2001] for a resolution on the abolition on the death penalty.

We hope to attain the goal of seeing the death penalty consigned to the history books as a form of punishment which has no place in the modern world.

The EU introduced the text, which calls on states to consider acceding to the Second Optional Protocol to the International Covenant on Civil and Political Rights. This instrument is aimed at abolishing the death penalty and to ensure that—in states where [the] death penalty has not yet been eradicated—it is only imposed for the most serious crimes and to establish a moratorium on executions. The resolution, amassing more than 60 co-sponsors, was adopted after a roll-call vote: of 53 CHR Members, 27 voted for, 18 against and 7 abstained.

The adoption of this resolution was needless to say the result of teamwork, very efficiently led by the EU Presidency, Sweden.

No Place in the Modern World

Another way for the Commission to pursue this policy is through EU assistance to programmes for promotion of human rights and democracy. Through mobilisation of public opinion against capital punishment we hope to attain the goal of seeing the death penalty consigned to the history books as a form of punishment which has no place in the modern world.

Funding such projects has recently been re-affirmed as a priority in the Commission's Communication, or policy paper, of 8 May 2001 on the Union's role in promoting human rights and democratisation in third countries.

The projects we support are often very practical. I would like to give you a couple of examples. One works with the University of the Philippines to increase use of DNA testing in capital cases. In the Philippines there are more than 1,000 death row convicts, most of whom lack the means to hire legal assistance. Challenging these death row convictions with DNA testing could greatly affect the current pro death penalty opinion.

We also fund projects to foster public awareness. We have a joint programme with the Council of Europe that originally covered Albania, the Russian Federation, Turkey and Ukraine. Since this programme was agreed, Ukraine has, however, abolished the death penalty. Maybe this proves the success of the programme!

The programme includes training for parliamentarians and other opinion makers on the practice in states that no longer practise the death penalty and how to speak persuasively to the public on these matters. It is well known that public opinion often demands that the death penalty be maintained and thus needs to receive information about the need to respect basic human rights.

There is still a long way to go. Let me just mention a few examples.

Dialogue on Human Rights

The figures emanating from China about its use of the death penalty under the 'strike hard' policy are so horrifying as to be almost unbelievable. It is therefore a central and regular element the EU-China human rights dialogue. Last April we discussed issues such as imposition of alternative sanctions to the death penalty.

In Iran, according to reports, the practice of executing women by stoning has recently been resumed [as of 2001]. This cruel method had not been applied since 1997. We have also learned that other women have recently been sentenced to execution through this method. It has therefore been necessary for me to raise this issue with my Iranian counterparts in recent meetings.

In relation to the US, EU activity aims at US withdrawal of its reservation concerning Article 6 of the International Covenant on Civil and Political rights. In addition, the EU has invited the US to respect the strict conditions for use of death penalty that are enumerated in several international instruments, notably in relation to juveniles and [the] mentally retarded.

These questions and others will certainly be among those discussed tomorrow under the specific agenda point on the US that will be chaired by Mr. Badinter.

I wish you fruitful discussions and congratulate all of you for your endeavours to obtain universal abolition of the death penalty.

10

Capital Punishment Does Not Make Nations Safer

Paul Simon

Until his death in 2003, Paul Simon was a professor at Southern Illinois University, where he taught classes in political science, history, and journalism, and served as director of the Public Policy Institute, which he founded. A Democrat from Illinois, he was elected to the U.S. House of Representatives in 1974 and the U.S. Senate in 1984, retiring in 1996.

It is not wise for the United States to have capital punishment. Other democratic societies consider the death penalty uncivilized, and capital punishment harms the United States' reputation as a human rights leader. Retaining capital punishment comes at a great cost—economically, morally, and judicially—and is not necessary to protect the country's citizens.

Just a couple of comments: one on the moral issue.

The field of theology and the field of faith grow. There is no condemnation in the Bible of capital punishment. There is no condemnation in the Bible of slavery. As a matter of fact, Saint Paul was quoted regularly from the book of Philemon in the defense of slavery, but gradually we have come to appreciate that slavery really is a moral issue. On the constitutional question, we also grow in that field. Now, there are dangers in that, obviously. You don't want to move from the fundamen-

Paul Simon, "A Call for Reckoning: Religion & the Death Penalty; Session Three: Religion, Politics, and the Death Penalty," *Pew Forum on Religion and Public Life*, January 25, 2002, pp. 11–13. Reproduced by permission of the author's literary estate.

tals, but *Plessy v. Ferguson*, 1896 . . . said, "separate but equal" doesn't violate the Constitution. We gradually came to realize that equal protection really had to say that we can't discriminate in school attendance, and then beyond school attendance into many other fields. But I think the basic question that we face is not: is it moral or is it unconstitutional; the question is, is it wise?

Simply Uncivilized

Let's take a look at who has the death penalty. Western Europe does not have the death penalty. When Turkey recently applied for admission to the European Union, the committee of the European Union that made a recommendation against Turkey's admission . . . gave as one of the two principal reasons that "Turkey retains the barbaric practice of capital punishment." Canada and Mexico have abandoned the death penalty. The European Parliament passed a resolution urging the United States to abandon the death penalty. An internationally circulated magazine says, "Throughout Europe in particular, the death penalty is thought of as simply uncivilized." The practice is thought to be particularly problematic for a leading nation. After all, German Justice Minister Herta Daeubler-Gmelin has argued, "The Americans do not hesitate, proud as they are of their democratic tradition, to reproach other countries over human rights violations."

I think the great cost is desensitizing us to death and to using violence as an instrument for civilized society.

Which nations are the great users of capital punishment? Well, in the year 2000—and the assumption is that China, where we don't have statistics, but that they had been the principal user of capital punishment. The second nation is Saudi Arabia. The third nation is the United States. The fourth nation is Iran. Since 1975, 35 retarded people have been executed; people whose IQ is below 70. Of the nations that have executed people for crimes committed below the age of 18 since 1990, they are these nations: Iran, Nigeria, Pakistan, Saudi Arabia, Yemen and the nation that has executed more than any others, the United States.

At Great Cost

It costs much more—I'm not suggesting that economics ought to dictate our decision on this, but as Beth Wilkinson [prosecutor in the Oklahoma City bombing trials for the terrorist attack of April 14, 1995] knows better than the rest of us, the Timothy McVeigh defense cost $13.8 million. For 10 percent of that amount, we could have held him in prison for the rest of his life. And you make heroes out of people. Shortly after the execution—and I remember being in Central Illinois and all of a sudden seeing someone with a T-shirt with Timothy McVeigh's picture on the T-shirt. Maybe that would have happened if he had been sentenced to life in prison. I don't know; I doubt it.

One study for the state of Illinois and the commission that Governor [George] Ryan appointed to look at capital punishment—I'm co-chairing that commission—we will get more up-to-date and perhaps more accurate information, but that it has cost the state of Illinois, over the last two-and-a half decades, $800 million more for executing people than for putting people in prison for life. But I think the great cost is desensitizing us to death and to using violence as an instrument for civilized society.

I think it's bad for the courts. The Constitution doesn't require, as [Supreme Court] Justice [Antonin] Scalia knows, doesn't require members of the Supreme Court to be lawyers. In fact, Justice Hugo Black suggests we ought to have one or two non-lawyers on the United States Supreme Court. . . . Justice Felix Frankfuter said this: "I am strongly against capital punishment for reasons that are not related to concern for the murderer or the risk of convicting the innocent. When life is at hazard in a trial, it sensationalizes the whole thing almost unwittingly. The effect on juries, the bar, the public, the judiciary, I regard as very bad."

Who gets capital punishment? Well, with rare exceptions, it's the poor who get capital punishment. If you have enough money, you don't get capital punishment. And Timothy McVeigh's situation is the rare exception where he certainly had adequate counsel, but that is a rarity. It is also discriminatory. If the victim is white, in the state of Florida you're 4.8 times more likely to get capital punishment; in Illinois, 4 times more likely; Oklahoma, 4.3 times more likely; Mississippi, 5.5 times more likely, and many other examples. In Kentucky, more than 1,000 African-Americans have been killed since 1975. All 39 death row inmates there, and those who have been executed, are there for killing a white person.

Feel Safer?

The whole question is, then, is it a deterrent? I asked a class a couple of years ago how many in the class favored capital punishment. An overwhelming percentage raised their hands. I asked them, how many think it is a deterrent? Not a single hand was raised. It's interesting that in England you had capital punishment, among other things, for pick-pocketing. They had public executions. And what was happening during these public executions? People were going around pick-pocketing in that audience.

We have to learn the lesson, not just in our country but anywhere—in the Middle East, anywhere, you name the area—violence breeds violence.

Is there anyone here who feels safer in Texas than in Iowa? Of the 12 states that do not have capital punishment, 10 are below the national average in the rate of murder. Of the seven states with the lowest murder rate, five don't have capital punishment. Twenty-seven states with the highest murder rate, all but two have it. Now, I'm not suggesting the way to reduce the murder rate is get rid of capital punishment. I suggest it is simply not a factor. Is there anyone here who feels less safe in North Dakota than in South Dakota? South Dakota has it; North Dakota doesn't have it. Or do you feel less safe in Massachusetts than in Connecticut? To ask the question is to answer it.

Innocent people are being put to death. We had the case in Illinois of Anthony Porter, two days away from execution [in December 1998], and the information came out he was not the person, and then he was freed by the courts. Since 1976, in Illinois, we have executed 12 people, and 13 people who have been on death row have been released because of DNA evidence that they were not guilty. I don't think there's any question that a great many people have been executed who were innocent. And I don't think we should be part of that. It's not necessary to protect our society.

And then, finally, I think we have to learn the lesson, not just in our country but anywhere—in the Middle East, anywhere, you name the area—violence breeds violence. Now, the state has to—from time to time—use force, but that force should not be excessive. And when it is excessive, then I think we do harm to society. The question is, is it wise to have capital punishment? And I think the evidence is overwhelming that it is not wise to have capital punishment.

11

The Islamic World Must Reexamine Capital Punishment

Tariq Ramadan

Tariq Ramadan is a professor of Islamic Studies and as of 2007 is a senior research fellow at Lokahi Foundation (London) and visiting fellow at St. Antony's College (Oxford). He is also president of the European Muslim Network, a think tank in Brussels, Belgium. Through his writings and lectures, he contributes to the debate on the issues of Muslims in the West and Islamic revival in the Muslim world.

Muslim societies implement the Islamic penal code in different ways, depending on their interpretation of their sacred texts, the Qur'an *(the holy scripture of Islam) and the* Sunna *(Islamic custom and practice based on the Prophet Muhammad's words and actions). The* ulamâ' *(Muslim scholars) recognize that the scriptures suggest the harsher punishment of* hudûd, *such as beating, stoning, and death, as a penalty for serious crimes. However, many* ulamâ' *believe that* hudûd *was meant to deter the individual from unacceptable, immoral behaviors by stirring that person's conscience, not by the literal application of the penalty. Although Islam is based on equality and justice, a majority of the Muslim population considers strict, harsh punishments more "Islamic" in character, especially in contrast to the perceived moral permissiveness of laws in the Western world. Mus-*

Tariq Ramadan, "An International Call for Moratorium on Capital Punishment, Stoning and the Death Penalty in the Islamic World," TariqRamadan.com, March 30, 2005. Reproduced by permission of the author.

lim men and women have a responsibility to challenge this popular support for corporal punishment and the death penalty, while remaining faithful to Islam.

Muslim majority societies and Muslims around the world are constantly confronted with the fundamental question of how to implement the penalties prescribed in the Islamic penal code.

Evoking the notion of *sharî'a*, or more precisely *hudûd*[1], the terms of the debate are defined by central questions emerging from thought provoking discussions taking place between *ulamâ'* (scholars) and/or Muslim masses: How to be faithful to the message of Islam in the contemporary era? How can a society truly define itself as "Islamic" beyond what is required in the daily practices of individual private life? But a critical and fruitful debate has not yet materialized.

Several currents of thought exist in the Islamic world today and disagreements are numerous, deep and recurring. Among these, a small minority demands the immediate and strict application of *hudûd*, assessing this as an essential prerequisite to truly defining a "Muslim majority society" as "*Islamic*". Others, while accepting the fact that the *hudûd* are indeed found in the textual references (the *Qur'an* and the *Sunna*[2], consider the application of *hudûd* to be conditional upon the state of the society which must be just and, for some, has to be "*ideal*" before these injunctions could be applied. Thus, the priority is the promotion of social justice, fighting against poverty and illiteracy etc. Finally, there are others, also a minority, who consider the texts relating to *hudûd* as obsolete and argue that these references have no place in contemporary Muslim societies.

1. A concept which literally means "limits". In the specialized language of Muslim jurists (*fuqahâ'*), this term is inclusive of the punishment which is revealed in the application of the Islamic Penal code. *Sharî'a*, literally "the way to the source" and a path to faithfulness, is a corpus of Islamic jurisprudence.
2. Prophetic tradition: texts which report what the Prophet of Islam (peace be upon him) did, said or approved of during his lifetime.

One can see the opinions on this subject are so divergent and entrenched that it becomes difficult to discern what the respective arguments are. At the very moment we are writing these lines—while serious debate is virtually non-existent, while positions remain vague and even nebulous, and consensus among Muslims is lacking—women and men are being subjected to the application of these penalties. For Muslims, Islam is a message of equality and justice. It is our faithfulness to the message of Islam that leads us to recognize that it [is] impossible to remain silent in the face of unjust applications of our religious references. The debate must liberate itself and refuse to be satisfied by general, timid and convoluted responses. These silences and intellectual contortions are unworthy of the clarity and just message of Islam.

The hudûd *would ... serve as a "deterrent," the objective of which would be to stir the conscience of the believer to the gravity of an action warranting such a punishment.*

In the name of the scriptural sources, the Islamic teachings, and the contemporary Muslim conscience, statements must be made and decisions need to be taken.

Hudûd as Internal Deterrent

All the *ulamâ'* (scholars) of the Muslim world, of yesterday and of today and in all the currents of thought, recognize the existence of scriptural sources that refer to corporal punishment (*Qur'an* and *Sunna*), stoning of adulterous men and women (*Sunna*) and the penal code (*Qur'an* and *Sunna*). The divergences between the *ulamâ'* and the various trends of thought (literalist, reformist, rationalist, etc.) are primarily rooted in the interpretation of a certain number of these texts, the conditions of application of the Islamic penal code, as well as its degree of relevance to the contemporary era (nature of the committed infractions, testimonials, social and political contexts, etc.).

The majority of the *ulamâ'*, historically and today, are of the opinion that these penalties are on the whole Islamic but that the conditions under which they should be implemented are nearly impossible to reestablish. These penalties, therefore, are "*almost never applicable*". The *hudûd* would, therefore, serve as a "deterrent," the objective of which would be to stir the conscience of the believer to the gravity of an action warranting such a punishment.

Anyone who reads the books of the *ulamâ'*, listens to their lectures and sermons, travels inside the Islamic world or interacts with the Muslim communities of the West will inevitably and invariably hear the following pronouncement from religious authorities: "*almost never applicable*". Such pronouncements give the majority of *ulamâ* and Muslim masses a way out of dealing with the fundamental issues and questions without risking appearing to have betrayed the Islamic scriptural sources. The alternative posture is to avoid the issue of *hudûd* altogether and/or to remain silent.

"Almost Never" Not the Reality

One would have hoped that this pronouncement, "*almost never*," would be understood as a[n] assurance that women and men would be protected from repressive and unjust treatment; one would have wished that the stipulated conditions would be seen, by legislators and government who claim Islam, as an imperative to promote equality before the law and justice among humans. Nothing could be further from the reality.

Behind an Islamic discourse that minimizes the reality and rounds off the angles, and within the shadows of this "*almost never*", lurks a somber reality where women and men are punished, beaten, stoned and executed in the name of *hudûd* while Muslim conscience the world over remains untouched.

It is as if one does not know, as though a minor violation is being done to the Islamic teachings. A still more grave injustice is that these penalties are applied almost exclusively to women and the poor, the doubly victimized, never to the wealthy, the powerful, or the oppressors. Furthermore, hundreds of prisoners have no access to anything that could even remotely be called defense counsel. Death sentences are decided and carried out against women, men and even minors (political prisoners, traffickers, delinquents, etc.) without [their] ever [being] given a chance to obtain legal counsel. In resigning ourselves to having a superficial relationship to the scriptural sources, we betray the message of justice of Islam.

The international community has an equally major and obvious responsibility to be involved in addressing the question of *hudûd* in the Muslim world. Thus far, the denunciations have been selective and calculated for the protection of geostrategic and economic interests. A poor country, in Africa or Asia, trying to apply the *hudûd* or the *sharî'a* will face the mobilization of international campaigns as we have seen recently. This is not the case with rich countries, the petromonarchies and those considered "allies". Towards the latter, denunciations are made reluctantly, or not at all, despite ongoing and acknowledged applications of these penalties typically carried out against the poorest or weakest segments of society. The intensity of the denouncements is inversely proportional to the interests at stake. A further injustice!

Harshness Is Not an Islamic Quality

For those who travel within the Islamic world and interact with Muslims, an analysis imposes itself: everywhere, populations are demonstrating an increasing devotion to Islam and its teachings. This reality, although interesting in itself, could be troubling, and even dangerous when the nature of this devotion is so fervent, where there is no real knowledge or comprehension of the texts, where there is so little if any critical distance vis-à-vis the different scholarly interpretations, the necessary contextualization, the nature of the required conditions or, indeed, the protection of the rights of the individual and the promotion of justice.

On the question of *hudûd*, one sometimes sees popular support hoping [for] or exacting a literal and immediate application because the latter would guarantee henceforth the "*Islamic*" character of a society. In fact, it is not rare to hear Muslim women and men (educated or not, and more often of modest means) calling for a formal and strict application of the penal code (in their mind, the *sharî'a)* of which they themselves will often be the first victims. When one studies this phenomenon, two types of reasoning generally motivate these claims:

1. The literal and immediate application of the *hudûd* legally and socially provides a visible reference to Islam. The legislation, by its harshness, gives the feeling of fidelity to the *Qur'anic* injunctions that demand rigorous respect of the text. At the popular level, one can infer in the African, Arabic, Asian as well as Western countries, that the very nature of this harshness and intransigence of the application, gives an Islamic dimension to the popular psyche.

2. The opposition and condemnations by the West supplies, paradoxically, the popular feeling of fidelity to the Islamic teachings; a reasoning that is antithetical, simple and simplistic. The intense opposition of the West is sufficient proof of the authentic Islamic character of the literal application of *hudûd*. Some will persuade themselves by asserting that the West has long since lost its moral references and become so permissive that the harshness of the Islamic penal code which punishes behaviors judged immoral, is by antithesis, the true and only alternative "*to Western decadence*".

These formalistic and binary [ways of] reasoning are fundamentally dangerous for they claim and grant an Islamic quality to a legislation, not in what it promotes, protects and applies justice to, but more so because it sanctions harsh and visible punishment to certain behaviors and in stark contrast and opposition to the Western laws, which are perceived as morally permissive and without a reference to religion[3]. One sees today that communities or Muslim people satisfy themselves with this type of legitimacy to back a government or a party that calls for an application of the *shari'a* narrowly understood as a literal and immediate application of corporal punishment, stoning and the death penalty.

Popular Passion Trumps Texts

When this type of popular passion takes hold, it is the first sign of a will to respond to various forms of frustration and humiliation by asserting an identity that perceives itself as Islamic (and anti-Western). Such an identity is not based on the comprehension of the objectives of the Islamic teachings (*al maqâsid*) or the different interpretations and conditions relating to the application of the *hudûd*.

Faced with this passion, many *ulamâ'* remain prudent for the fear of losing their credibility with the masses. One can observe a psychological pressure exercised by this popular sentiment towards the judicial process of the *ulamâ'*, which normally should be independent so as to educate the population and propose alternatives. Today, an inverse phenomenon is revealing itself. The majority of the *ulamâ'* are afraid to confront these popular and simplistic claims which lack knowledge, are passionate and binary, for fear of losing their status and being defined as having compromised too much, not been strict enough, too westernized or not Islamic enough.

---

3. In Muslim countries, laws that we see as being "borrowed from the west" are often interpreted as tools by dictatorial governments to mislead and legitimize their autocratic character, and more importantly, to promote a westernized culture and morals.

The *ulamâ'*, who should be the guarantors of a deep reading of the texts, the guardians of fidelity to the objectives of justice and equality and of the critical analysis of conditions and social contexts, find themselves having to accept either a formalistic application (an immediate non-contextualized application), or a binary reasoning (less West is more Islam), or hide behind *"almost never applicable"* pronouncements which protects them but which does not provide real solutions to the daily injustices experienced by women and the poor.

An Impossible *Status Quo*

The Islamic world is experiencing a very deep crisis the causes of which are multiple and sometimes contradictory. The political system of the Arab world is becoming more and more entrenched, references to Islam frequently instrumentalized, and public opinion is often muzzled or blindly passionate (to such a point as to accept, indeed even to call for, the most repressive interpretations and least just application of the *"Islamic sharî'a"* and *hudûd*).

In terms of the more circumscribed religious question, we can observe a crisis of authority accompanied by an absence of internal debate among the *ulamâ'* in the diverse schools of thought and within Muslim societies. It becomes apparent that a variety of opinions, accepted in Islam, are whirling today within a chaotic framework leading to the coexistence of disparate and contradictory Islamic legal opinions each claiming to have more *"Islamic character"* than the other.

Faced with this legal chaos, the ordinary Muslim public is more appeased by *"an appearance of fidelity"*, than it is persuaded by opinions based on real knowledge and understanding of the governing Islamic principles and rules *(ahkâm)*.

Let us look at the reality, as it exists. There is today a quadruple crisis of closed and repressive political systems, religious authorities upholding contradictory juristic positions and unknowledgeable populations swept up in remaining faithful to the teachings of Islam through religious fervor than through true reflection. The crisis cannot legitimize our silence. We are accomplices and guilty when women and men are punished, stoned or executed in the name of a formal application of the scriptural sources.

The Muslim Responsibility

It leaves the responsibility to the Muslims of the entire world. It is for them to rise to the challenge of remaining faithful to the message of Islam in the contemporary era; it is for them to denounce the failures and the betrayals being carried out by whatever authorities or any Muslim individual. A prophetic tradition reports: "Support your brother, whether he be unjust or victim of an injustice." One of the Companions asked: "Messenger of God, I understand how to support someone that is a victim of injustice, but how can I support him who is unjust?" The Prophet (peace be upon him) responded: "Prevent him from being unjust, that is [how] you support to him."[4]

It thus becomes the responsibility of each 'âlim (scholar), of each conscience, every woman and man, wherever they may be to speak up. Western Muslims either hide behind the argument that they are exempt from the application of the sharî'a or hudûd since they are "in a minority position"[5]. Their avoidance of the questions leaves a heavy and troubling silence. Or they express condemnation from afar without attempting to change the situation and influence the mentalities. These Muslim women and men who live in places of political freedom, who have access to education and knowledge—in the very name of the Islamic teachings—have a major responsibility to attempt to reform the situation, open a relevant debate, condemn and put a[n] end to injustices perpetrated in their name.

4. Hadîth reported by al-Bukhârî and Muslim.
5. The argument is weak and dangerous as it tacitly accepts the application of hudûd within today's societal context as "Islamic."

12

The United States Must Reconsider the Death Penalty

Richard C. Dieter

Richard C. Dieter is executive director of the Death Penalty Information Center. A graduate of Georgetown University Law Center, he is also an adjunct professor at the Catholic University Law School.

International opposition to the death penalty is beginning to influence the United States' position on capital punishment. The United States recognizes the increasing need for cooperation among countries in the promotion of human rights, international trade and development, and fighting terrorism. When U.S. allies are reluctant to extradite suspected terrorists because of the possibility of execution, for example, this negatively impacts not only the war on terror, but also the United States' reputation and standing in world opinion. The United States cannot risk becoming isolated and must reconsider its use of the death penalty.

Slowly, but impressively, international law and opinion are beginning to have an impact on law in the United States, and particularly on the death penalty. While the law and practices of other countries may not have played a significant role in the past in the evaluation of our society's standards of decency, recent opinions indicate that that influence may be growing. And while the American public strongly supported

Richard C. Dieter, "International Influence on the Death Penalty in the U.S." *Foreign Service Journal*, vol. 80, October 2003, pp. 31–38. Copyright © American Foreign Service Association 2003. Reproduced by permission.

the death penalty during periods when many of this country's closest allies were renouncing capital punishment, public opinion in the U.S. is now shifting. The prospects for profound change in the death penalty in the U.S. are stronger now than at any other time in the long and controversial history of this important issue.

There are at least three reasons for this development. First, there is a greater recognition of the need for international cooperation and respect for the laws of other democracies, and this recognition is finding its way into decisions by the highest courts in the U.S. Second, today there is a broader intersection between U.S. capital punishment law and the interests of other countries. Issues of extradition, the execution of foreign nationals, and the prospects of military tribunals to deal with suspected foreign terrorists often put the death penalty and international human rights concerns in direct conflict. Third, while the past presented the U.S. with a diversity of views on capital punishment among its allies, the present confronts us with a near unanimity on certain aspects of the death penalty and a growing consensus condemning its use in general.

International Influence in the Past

The death penalty in the earliest days of the United States was a continuation of the practice brought over from England, but less harsh. The number of crimes punishable by death was curtailed in the early colonies compared to the long list of capital offenses in England, and gradually became limited to the most violent crimes such as first degree murder and rape. Some jurisdictions in the U.S. abolished the death penalty in their state systems long before that became the norm in Western Europe. The state of Michigan abolished the death penalty in 1846 and Wisconsin took a similar step in 1853. Neither state has carried out an execution since then.

But the death penalty was not seriously challenged as a constitutional issue in the U.S. until the late 1960s—a time of considerable turmoil on civil rights issues here, and a time of movement toward abolition of the death penalty in Europe. This challenge resulted in the somewhat surprising decision of the U.S. Supreme Court in *Furman v. Georgia* in 1972 finding the death penalty to be unconstitutional as it was being applied everywhere in the U.S. The five opinions of the concurring justices made scant mention of any trend away from the death penalty outside the U.S., though they recognized the debt that the ban on cruel and unusual punishments owed to English law and the Magna Carta. Some of the justices measured the meaning of this clause by the "evolving standards of decency" in society, but did not look to other countries for these standards.

The decisive rationale for holding the death penalty unconstitutional in *Furman* rested on its arbitrary and capricious use within the United States, rather than on any declining use or condemnation from abroad. In fact, a number of the justices pointed to the increasing rarity of the use of the death penalty in the U.S. as a reason for stopping it all together. Justice [Potter] Stewart, one of the two key justices in the decision, compared the death penalty to the random act of being "struck by lightning." Justice [Byron] White, the other centrist, said that it was impossible to distinguish the many cases eligible for the death penalty from the few who received it.

International influence on the U.S. death penalty perhaps reached its nadir in the dispute over the execution of foreign nationals in this country.

In the late 1980s, international opinion was considered but largely rejected in the discussion of the death penalty for juvenile offenders. The Supreme Court banned the execution of those who were under 16 years-of-age at the time of their offense in *Thompson v. Oklahoma* in 1988, relying almost exclusively on U.S. practice at the time. When the Court was faced with the companion question regarding the execution of those who were 16 or 17 years old at the time of their crime, it not only allowed the practice, but Justice [Antonin] Scalia, writing for the court, strongly objected to the use of international opinion in evaluating the evolving standards of decency to apply in the U.S., a point raised by the dissent. This sharp difference of opinion on the use of international standards set the stage for future battles on the death penalty in the Court.

The Execution of Foreign Nationals

International influence on the U.S. death penalty perhaps reached its nadir in the dispute over the execution of foreign nationals in this country. When it was gradually discovered that the U.S. had been systematically ignoring the provisions of the Vienna Convention on Consular Relations by failing to inform defendants of their right to confer with their respective consulates, and that some of these defendants had been sentenced to death, numerous objections were raised. . . .

In the past, the issue received scant attention until executions of such persons began occurring regularly in the 1990s. Even then, the raising of the Vienna Convention as a legal challenge to the death penalty was rare. There was little knowledge of how many foreign nationals were present on death row, and from what countries. Today, all that has changed. Both defense attorneys in the U.S. and officials from other countries are aware of this issue and that there are at least 118 foreign nationals from 30 different countries on death rows across the U.S. [as of 2003].

In addition to the execution of foreign nationals, there are numerous instances where people wanted for crime in the U.S. are arrested in other countries. The question of extradition and the possible use of the death penalty has raised major concerns throughout Europe, Canada, Mexico, and parts of Africa. The urgency of this issue has been heightened by the events of Sept. 11 and the war on terrorism. Suspected terrorists not only may face the death penalty in the U.S. if extradited, but they may also be tried in a military tribunal that lacks the normal due process afforded defendants in the civilian courts. While the U.S. sorely wants to bring such suspects to justice, many countries just as strongly believe that the death penalty is a human rights issue and extradition in such circumstances would be a violation of deeply held principles.

In the face of such consistent and adamant challenges to the death penalty, the U.S. risks becoming isolated at a time when it can least afford it.

In a measure of the direct influence that countries can have when they hold something the U.S. wants, states and the federal government have agreed to drop the prospect of capital punishment in numerous cases in exchange for extradition from other countries. Similarly, following a visit by British Prime Minister Tony Blair to Washington ... [in July 2003], the U.S. announced that the death penalty would not be sought against two British citizens who were among the first six to be tried under the new military tribunals. It appears that a similar rule will apply against two Australian citizens who have also been held at Guantanamo Bay, Cuba, awaiting military tribunals.

A More Cohesive Opposition

Clearly, the world is more interconnected than ever before. Interests of trade, the promotion of human rights, fighting terrorism, and international development, all require greater cooperation among countries. The U.S. is keenly aware of these new realities and has sought allies for its military interventions in Kuwait, Afghanistan, and Iraq. The U.S. concern was also demonstrated by its angry reaction to being excluded from the U.N. Commission on Human Rights in 2001 (though it has now regained its seat). The U.S. is facing a further embarrassment if it loses its observer status in the Council of Europe, which has been directly tied to movement on the death penalty issue.

In the long run, the reason why international opposition to the death penalty may finally be having a significant impact on the U.S. is that this opposition is more cohesive than ever before. The United States' closest allies in Europe and North America are unanimous in rejecting the death penalty and they do not hesitate to let their views be known. New countries can only be admitted to the growing European Union, a body whose size and economy may soon equal or surpass the U.S., if they renounce the death penalty. Courts in countries such as Canada and Mexico, and throughout Europe, have begun to consistently refuse extradition as long as the death penalty is a possibility in the U.S. And, on the issue of the execution of juvenile offenders, every country of the world, with the possible exception of Somalia, has ratified the Convention on the Rights of the Child forbidding such executions. In the face of such consistent and adamant challenges to the death penalty, the U.S. risks becoming isolated at a time when it can least afford it.

There are increasing signs that giving way on the death penalty would not be the major concession it would have been in the past. Doubts about the accuracy and fairness of the death penalty have increased dramatically in the U.S. as scores of inmates have been freed from death row. Support for life without parole sentences has increased, and the number of death sentences in the U.S. has plummeted by 50 percent in recent years. The only contrary trend is a more aggressive use of the federal death penalty by the present administration. But even there, the results reflect a growing ambivalence about this ultimate sentence: 20 of the last 21 federal capital prosecutions have resulted in sentences of less than death.

International concerns about the death penalty would probably never be enough alone to make the U.S. abandon this practice. But capital punishment is unlikely to be undone for any one reason. Like snow on a branch, it is not any single flake that makes the branch break, but rather the collective weight of many flakes accumulating over time. Because international concerns are generally being given more recognition in the U.S., because various aspects of the U.S. death penalty are forcibly intersecting with the citizens and principles of other countries, and because the opinion of those other countries is more unified than ever before, it is likely that the death penalty will come under increasing criticism both here and abroad, and its use will continue to decline.

13

Executions Send a Strong Deterrent Message

Peter Ryan

Peter Ryan is an Australian author of numerous books, articles, newspaper columns, reviews, and criticism. He was director of Melbourne University Press from 1962 to 1989 and an officer of the Victorian Supreme Court.

A minority of the Australian population—typically those who consider themselves progressive and better educated than the general public—oppose capital punishment and consider it barbaric. The abolitionists also raise the disturbing possibility that an innocent person may be put to death, although an improved appeals process makes these cases rare. The majority of the population, by contrast, senses that some crimes are so heinous that the perpetrators should be cut off from society, with death as the only appropriate punishment. The execution of such individuals can deter others from committing similar crimes, saving innocent lives.

> *I went out to Charing Cross, to see Major-general Harrison hanged, drawn and quartered; which was done there, he looking as cheerful as any man could do in that condition.*

The author of those words was no sadistic voyeur, but [seventeenth-century English diarist] Samuel Pepys, as humane and genial a man as ever lived. Clearly, his view of capital punishment differed a good deal from the heated criti-

Peter Ryan, "Capital Punishment," *Quadrant*, vol. 50, January–February 2006, p. 127. Copyright 2006 Quadrant Magazine Company, Inc. Reproduced by permission of the publisher and author.

cism which has lately filled the Australian media. Indeed, from Pepys's description of the unlucky Harrison, perhaps even the condemned person saw things differently in those days.

As so often is the case when a truly serious question requires careful thought and calm debate, ... [the December 2005] Singapore incident [in which Vietnamese Australian Van Tuong Nguyen was convicted of drug trafficking and executed by hanging in Singapore] was hijacked by the excited voices of the ineffably pure-hearted and self-righteous. I think it was [British author, journalist, and satirist] Auberon Waugh who first named them "the chattering classes"—an imperfect label, true, but probably still the best short collective term we have. It includes (from time to time and according to taste) those who are "better-educated", elites, bleeding hearts, greens, do-gooders, enthusiasts, monomaniacs, progressives, journalists, academics, lawyers, clergy, ABC [Australian Broadcasting Company] hacks; in short, all "right-thinking persons". Many of them are good and intelligent, and far more virtuous than I am. Often, their arguments (more frequently parts of their arguments) deserve respect.

But, like the deafening colony of fruit bats infesting the gum trees outside, they make themselves intolerable with their shrill conviction that they are necessarily right; that we are backward peasants; that they command a majority of public opinion or (if they don't) that their purity of heart entitles them to override the true balance of democratic preference (that is, whatever it might be that all the rest of us happen to think). This sinister mindset [English author] George Orwell identified as the root of intellectual authoritarianism.

"Chattering Classes" the Minority

They are slow learners, these chatterers; the lesson above all which they resist is that they are a minority, and that only the parrot-like support of their close cousins in the media confirms their delusions of grandeur. Can anything shock them into facing reality? They revile [Australian prime minister] John Howard unceasingly, yet the mass of voters re-elect him at every opportunity they get.

Realists, for example, gave [Australian opposition leader] Mark Latham not the faintest chance of winning the election of October 2004. And no one who saw it will ever forget the stunned-mullet look on the ABC face of [Australian journalist] Kerry O'Brien on election-eve Friday: the polls had just shown him that Mark Latham had already gurgled down the plughole of the morrow's election. My barber, my barman and my fruiterer were shrewder judges than O'Brien.

District officers . . . stamped out head-hunting by the expedient of a few-score exemplary hangings, saving by this economical means the lives of a multitude of innocent men, women and babies.

On scattered rafts, these chatterers drift daily into the distance on some limitless postmodern ocean; but Australia, in the immortal phrase of [American comedian] Groucho Marx, "is someplace else".

But back to hanging or, rather, to capital punishment, in whatsoever form death may be inflicted.

Capital Punishment the Norm

I suppose my generation absorbed the broad idea of capital punishment as simply normal: [sixteenth-century English king] Henry VIII chopped the heads off errant wives and inconvenient clergymen, and [seventeenth-century British king] Charles I was beheaded for reasons which today seem amazingly narrow-minded; [English novelist] Charles Dickens taught us that Madame Defarge [a ruthless character in Dickens's *A Tale of Two Cities* who supports the French Revolution] kept her coded lists for the guillotine. We cheered the Royal Navy as it cleansed the oceans of piracy and slavery through regular hangings at the yard-arm; [nineteenth-century Australian outlaw and folk hero] Ned Kelly met bravely the proper fate ordained for him by law. In Papua and in New Guinea, practical-minded District Officers (under more than one of whom I was proud to serve) stamped out head-hunting by the expedient of a few-score exemplary hangings, saving by this economical means the lives of a multitude of innocent men, women and babies.

In 1942, at the almost grotesquely geriatric age of eighteen, I was appointed under martial law to be a magistrate of a New Guinea court with power to impose sentence of death. Punishment might not be carried into execution without the personal confirmation in writing of the Commander-in-Chief, General [Sir Thomas Albert] Blarney. I remain grateful that no case before me ever went so far as to require the least attention by the General, but the very existence of such a power was enough to concentrate a young man's mind wonderfully on reflective hot nights in the bush.

Back in civil life, I early read what were then the leading liberal texts on capital punishment, all of them by authors whom I continue greatly to admire: [British writer] Arthur Koestler, [French novelist, essayist, and dramatist] Albert Camus's "Reflections on the Guillotine", George Orwell's "A Hanging". Last week I re-read them all; what force do they exert today?

My impression was that Koestler, though all the clarity and cogency remained, had lost some of the urgency of his persuasion. I noted that Camus diluted his moral strength by branching out into a subordinate argument which said, in effect: "Okay, well, if we insist on retaining capital punishment, let's find a method more humane than our dreadful guillotine." And he descends then almost into Grand Guignol [horror drama of a macabre nature featuring graphic violence] in efforts to discredit—not capital punishment—but his country's particular method of despatch.

Orwell's "A Hanging", this time around, remained a transfixing and accurate depiction of the tension and horror which attends the hanging of a human. But you will read it in vain for argument against capital punishment as such; substitute, say, an intravenous needle for the rope, and Orwell's essay simply vanishes.

Contemplating Abolition

The Victorian lawyer family of Galbally were famous for their lifelong campaign against capital punishment. John Galbally, Labor member of Victoria's Legislative Council, over nearly twenty years introduced annually his own private member's bill to abolish hanging. In the 1950s, before television went coloured, and viewers goggled at grainy black-and-white, I debated the subject on HSV7 with Frank Galbally, that formidable advocate and passionate anti-hanger who died . . . [in October 2005].

In 1962 and again in 1966 I was deeply (and I hope not unhelpfully) involved in campaigns to avert the gallows for two condemned men, one in Melbourne and one in Perth, whom I believed had been unjustly convicted.

If all these autobiographical snippets are tedious, they have been set down to persuade readers that, however different their own views may be, mine have at least been reached after a lifetime of steady and (sometimes) close-quarters contemplation.

How can anyone possibly know how many potential murderers have been deterred by the prospect of their own death as a consequence?

Several of the arguments for abolition are powerful, as far as they go. A person wrongly hanged has been despatched forever beyond all compensation or amend, and the guilt remains a stain on society. And it has happened—look at Timothy Evans in London [Evans, wrongly convicted of the 1949 murders of his wife and daughter, was hanged in 1950]; improved processes of appeal make a repetition almost impossible.

The very existence of the death penalty may tend to pervert the course of justice; no matter how horrible the crime, and no matter how clear the proof of guilt, some jurors simply will not convict if there is the remotest chance that a hanging might follow. How such jurors square their consciences with their oath to find a true verdict escapes me, but their duplicity would certainly be condoned by the more fanatical of today's anti-hangers.

Executions Send Message

The abolitionist argument that hanging does not deter is not quite honest. How can anyone possibly know how many potential murderers have been deterred by the prospect of their own death as a consequence? Four or five years ago, in Victoria, the conservative parties flew a kite on the restoration of the death penalty, but did not proceed. But Papua New Guinea, having abolished hanging, was obliged to restore it in 1989, as a deterrent to a rising tide of violent crime.

Punishment of death should remain as an earnest of integrity, as proof that we mean what we say.

Ceaseless as those fruit bats, the chatterers repeat their cry that any society which uses the death penalty stands automatically condemned: backward, barbaric, cruel, immoral, subhuman and generally malignant. Among the vast populations of our Asian neighbours, this attitude reveals Australians as a precariously tiny minority, and patronising at that, with a substantial proportion of self-righteous prigs.

But, just as fruit bats hang upside-down, the truth is the other way round. In a moral and humane society citizens know in their bones that there are limits beyond which wickedness may not transgress, and that crimes sufficiently foul will cut off even membership of society. The abolition of hanging does not necessarily show respect for human life. It may just as easily betray contempt for the lives of slaughtered innocents, combined with irrational tenderness for the lives of the wicked who have cut them off. The worst cases of atrocious crime (including especially promiscuous acts of terrorism) should attract the possibility of execution when no extenuation can be shown.

I do not expect that we should keep a hangman heavily employed; indeed, I hope that his job would be a near-sinecure [steady payment for a job rarely performed]. But punishment of death should remain as an earnest of integrity, as proof that we mean what we say.

The humanitarian Camus understood this. Even as he campaigned for the abolition of the guillotine in France, he worried about "that modern tendency to absolve everything ... such sentimentality is made up of cowardice rather than of generosity".

Among the opponents of the death penalty I recognise and respect some whose conviction rises from deep and thoughtful moral principle. Many others—just tackle a few of them in argument yourself—enjoy an inexpensive sense of superior virtue, simply by attacking the laws of other countries. Their "principles" rest only on Camus's "cowardice" or (put another way) on mere squeamishness that, even in imagination, cannot face the sound of a sharply snapping criminal neck.

Organizations to Contact

The editors have compiled the following list of organizations concerned with the issues debated in this book. The descriptions are derived from materials provided by the organizations. All have publications or information available for interested readers. The list was compiled on the date of publication of the present volume; the information provided here may change. Be aware that many organizations take several weeks or longer to respond to inquiries, so allow as much time as possible.

American Civil Liberties Union (ACLU)
125 Broad St., 18th Floor, New York, NY   10004
(888) 567-2258 • fax: (212) 549-2646
Web site: www.aclu.org

The ACLU believes that capital punishment violates the Constitution's ban on cruel and unusual punishment as well as the requirements of due process and equal protection under the law. It publishes and distributes numerous books, pamphlets, reports, and position papers, including "Mental Illness and the Death Penalty in the United States" and *How the Death Penalty Weakens U.S. National Interests*. The Capital Punishment Project (CPP), a national project of the ACLU, challenges the unfairness and arbitrariness of capital punishment while working toward its ultimate repeal.

Amnesty International USA (AI)
5 Penn Plaza, New York, NY   10001
(212) 807-8400 • fax: (212) 627-1451
e-mail: aimember@aiusa.org
Web site: www.amnestyusa.org

Amnesty International (AI) is an independent worldwide movement working impartially for the release of all prisoners of conscience, fair and prompt trials for political prisoners, and an end to torture and executions. AI's Program to Abolish the Death Penalty (PADP) coordinates efforts to build coalitions with grassroots activists and social justice organizations working toward the elimination of the death penalty worldwide. AI's Web site includes links to news releases, fact sheets, and reports, including "Prisoner-assisted Homicide—More 'Volunteer' Executions Loom."

Campaign to End the Death Penalty (CEDP)
PO Box 25730, Chicago, IL   60625
(773) 955-4841 • fax: (773) 955-4841
Web site: www.nodeathpenalty.org

CEDP is a national, membership-driven, chapter-based grassroots organization dedicated to the abolition of capital punishment in the United States. It works to give a voice to death row prisoners and their family members. Publications include fact sheets and the CEDP's newsletter, *The New Abolitionist.*

Catholics Against Capital Punishment (CACP)
PO Box 5706, Bethesda, MD   20824-5706
fax: (301) 654-0925
e-mail: ellen.frank@verizon.net
Web site: www.cacp.org

CACP was founded in 1992 to promote greater awareness of Catholic Church teachings that characterize capital punishment as unnecessary, inappropriate, and unacceptable. It disseminates news of Catholic-oriented anti-death penalty efforts through its newsletter, *CACP News Notes,* and its Web site.

Citizens United for Alternatives to the Death Penalty (CUADP)
PMB 335, 2603 Dr. Martin Luther King Jr. Hwy.
Gainesville, FL   32609
(800) 973-6548
e-mail: cuadp@cuadp.org
Web site: www.cuadp.org

CUADP works to end the death penalty in the United States through aggressive campaigns of public education and the promotion of tactical grassroots activism. Its Web site includes death penalty and execution news and updates, press releases, and links to suggested readings. Students researching the death penalty for a class project may submit specific questions or interview requests to infodesk@cuadp.org.

Criminal Justice Legal Foundation (CJLF)
PO Box 1199, Sacramento, CA   95812
(916) 446-0345
Web site: www.cjlf.org

Established in 1982 as a nonprofit public interest law organization, the CJLF seeks to restore a balance between the rights of crime victims and the criminally accused. The foundation supports the death penalty and works to reduce the length, complexity, and expense of appeals as well as to improve law enforcement's ability to identify and prosecute criminals. Its Web site offers reports on pending cases and links to studies and articles about capital punishment.

Death Penalty Focus (DPF)
870 Market St., Ste. 859, San Francisco, CA   94102
(415) 243-0143 • fax: (415) 243-0994
e-mail: information@deathpenalty.org
Web site: www.deathpenalty.org

Founded in 1988, Death Penalty Focus is a nonprofit organization dedicated to the abolition of capital punishment through grassroots organizing, research, and the dissemination of information about the death penalty and its alternatives. It publishes an information bulletin, *The Catalyst*, as well as a quarterly newsletter, *The Sentry*.

Death Penalty Information Center (DPIC)
1101 Vermont Ave., NW, Ste. 701, Washington, DC   20005
(202) 289-2275 • fax: (202) 289-7336
e-mail: dpic@deathpenaltyinfo.org
Web site: www.deathpenaltyinfo.org

DPIC conducts research into public opinion on the death penalty. The center believes capital punishment is discriminatory and excessively costly and that it may result in the execution of innocent persons. It publishes numerous reports, such as *Blind Justice: Juries Deciding Life and Death with Only Half the Truth, Innocence and the Crisis in the American Death Penalty,* and *International Perspectives on the Death Penalty: A Costly Isolation for the U.S.,* in addition to the DPIC year-end reports. The DPIC Web site features a searchable database for executions, recent news releases, editorials, articles, statements, video clips, and more.

Derechos Human Rights
46 Estabrook St., San Leandro, CA 94577
(510) 483-4005
e-mail: hr@derechos.org
Web site: www.derechos.org

Derechos Human Rights is an international, independent, nonprofit organization that promotes human rights and works against violations to humanitarian law all over the world. The organization recognizes that while most civilized nations consider the death penalty as cruel and unusual punishment, it is not against customary international law, and debate on its application continues. Derechos Human Rights' Web site includes links to death penalty resources, such as Web sites, blogs, writings from death row prisoners, reports, and articles. It publishes the Human Rights Blog.

Equal Justice USA
The Quixote Center, Hyattsville, MD 20782
(301) 699-0042 • fax: (301) 864-2182
e-mail: ejusa@quixote.org
Web site: www.ejusa.org

Launched in 1990 as a grassroots project of the Quixote Center, Equal Justice USA mobilizes and educates citizens around issues of crime and punishment, bringing into focus the racial, economic, and political biases of the U.S. legal system. Equal Justice USA highlights the inequities in the death penalty and works toward abolishing it. It operates three programs, *Moratorium Now!,* the Grassroots Investigation Project, and the DC Books to Prisons Project. Publications include *Reasonable Doubts: Is the U.S. Executing Innocent People?* and *Capital Defense Handbook for Defendants and Their Families.*

Justice Fellowship (JF)
44180 Riverside Parkway, Lansdowne, VA   20176
(877) 478-0100
Web site: www.justicefellowship.org

Justice Fellowship is an online community of Christians working to reform the criminal justice system so that it reflects biblically based principles of restorative justice. Founded in 1983 as a subsidiary of Prison Fellowship Ministries, JF seeks to recognize the needs of crime victims and their families and hold offenders accountable to society. It does not take a position on the death penalty, but it publishes essays on capital punishment such as *A Call to Dialogue on Capital Punishment* and *The Question Is: What Is Just?*

Murder Victims' Families for Human Rights (MVFHR)
2161 Massachusetts Ave., Cambridge, MA   02140
(617) 491-9600
e-mail: info@murdervictimsfamilies.org
Web site: http://murdervictimsfamilies.org

MVFHR is an international, nongovernmental organization of family members of victims of criminal murder, terrorist killings, state executions, extrajudicial assassinations, and "disappearances" working to oppose the death penalty from a human rights perspective. Its activities include legislative action, speaking, and education. It publishes a newsletter, annual reports, and other reports such as *Creating More Victims: How Executions Hurt the Families Left Behind.*

Murder Victims' Families for Reconciliation, Inc. (MVFR)
2100 M St. NW, Ste. 170-296, Washington, DC   20037
(877) 896-4702
e-mail: info@mvfr.org
Web site: www.mvfr.org

Founded in 1976, MVFR is a national organization of family members who have lost a loved one to execution or murder and who oppose the death penalty. Members believe that capital trials divert resources from victim services to law enforcement, and the organization seeks to help policymakers, the press, and the public understand the negative impact of capital punishment on the families of victims and the condemned. MVFR's publications include *Dignity Denied: The Experience of Murder Victims' Family Members Who Oppose the Death Penalty, Not in Our Name,* and the quarterly MVFR newsletter, *Raising Our Voices.*

National Coalition to Abolish the Death Penalty (NCADP)
1705 DeSales St. NW, 5th Floor, Washington, DC   20036
(202) 331-4090 • fax: (202) 331-4099
e-mail: info@ncadp.org
Web site: www.ncadp.org

The NCADP is a national organization exclusively devoted to abolishing capital punishment in the United States. The coalition provides information, advocates for public policy, and mobilizes and supports individuals and institutions that share its unconditional rejection of capital punishment. To further its goals, the NCADP compiles statistics on the death penalty and publishes *Lifelines,* information packets, pamphlets, and research materials. Its Web site includes press releases, news archives, legislative action links, and execution alerts.

National Criminal Justice Reference Service (NCJRS)
PO Box 6000, Rockville, MD   20849-6000
(800) 851-3420 • fax: (301) 519-5212
Web site: www.ncjrs.org

Administered by the Office of Justice Programs, U.S. Department of Justice, the federally funded National Criminal Justice Reference Service is one of the most extensive sources of information on criminal and juvenile justice in the world. For a nominal fee, this clearinghouse provides topical searches and reading lists on many areas of criminal justice, including the death penalty. It publishes an annual report on capital punishment.

Religious Organizing Against the Death Penalty Project
c/o Criminal Justice Program, Philadelphia, PA   19102
(215) 241-7130 • fax: (215) 241-7119
e-mail: information@deathpenaltyreligious.org
Web site: www.deathpenaltyreligious.org

The Religious Organizing Against the Death Penalty Project seeks to build a powerful coalition of faith-based advocates. Nationally, it works with official religious bodies to develop strategies and to promote anti–death penalty activism within each faith tradition. Resources include a compilation of statements of opposition to capital punishment from faith groups, the booklet *Sermons, Homilies, and Reflections on the Death Penalty*, study guides, educational videos, and links to related articles.

Southern Center for Human Rights
83 Poplar St., NW, Atlanta, GA   30303-2122
(404) 688-1202 • fax: (404) 688-9440
Web site: www.schr.org

The Southern Center for Human Rights is a nonprofit, public interest law firm dedicated to enforcing the civil and human rights of people in the criminal justice system in the South. The Center's death penalty project challenges discrimination against people of color, the poor, and the disadvantaged in the application of the death penalty through litigation, community involvement, and public education. It publishes numerous articles and reports, including "Will the Death Penalty Remain Alive in the Twenty-First Century?: International Norms, Discrimination, Arbitrariness and the Risk of Executing the Innocent" and "The Death Penalty: Casualties and Costs of the War on Crime."

Bibliography

Books

James R. Acker, Robert M. Bohm, and Charles S. Lanier, eds.
America's Experiment with Capital Punishment: Reflections on the Past, Present, and Future of the Ultimate Penal Sanction, 2nd ed. Durham, NC: Carolina Academic Press, 2003.

James R. Acker and David Reep Karp, eds.
Wounds That Do Not Bind: Victim-based Perspectives on the Death Penalty. Durham, NC: Carolina Academic Press, 2006.

Laura Argys and Naci Mocan
Who Shall Live and Who Shall Die?: An Analysis of Prisoners on Death Row in the United States. Cambridge, MA: National Bureau of Economic Research, 2003.

Stuart Banner
The Death Penalty: An American History. Cambridge, MA: Harvard University Press, 2002.

Hugo Adam Bedau
Killing as Punishment: Reflections on the Death Penalty in America. Boston: Northeastern University Press, 2004.

Hugo Adam Bedau and Paul G. Cassell, eds.
Debating the Death Penalty: Should America Have Capital Punishment? The Experts on Both Sides Make Their Best Case. New York: Oxford University Press, 2004.

John D. Bessler — *Kiss of Death: America's Love Affair with the Death Penalty.* Boston: Northeastern University Press, 2003.

Joan Cheever — *Back from the Dead: One Woman's Search for the Men Who Walked off America's Death Row.* Hoboken, NJ: Wiley, 2006.

Stanley Cohen — *The Wrong Men: America's Epidemic of Wrongful Death Row Convictions.* New York: Carroll & Graf Publishers, 2003.

Mike Gray — *The Death Game: Capital Punishment and the Luck of the Draw.* Monroe, ME: Common Courage Press, 2003.

Craig Haney — *Death by Design: Capital Punishment as a Social Psychological System.* New York: Oxford University Press, 2005.

Bill Kurtis — *The Death Penalty on Trial: Crisis in American Justice.* New York: Public Affairs, 2004.

Evan J. Mandery — *Capital Punishment: A Balanced Examination.* Sudbury, MA: Jones and Bartlett Publishers, 2005.

Charles F. Ogletree Jr. and Austin Sarat, eds. — *From Lynch Mobs to the Killing State: Race and the Death Penalty in America.* New York: New York University Press, 2006.

Sister Helen Prejean — *The Death of Innocents.* New York: Random House, 2005.

Austin Sarat and Christian Boulanger, eds. — *The Cultural Lives of Capital Punishment: Comparative Perspectives.* Palo Alto, CA: Stanford University Press, 2005.

Richard A. Stack — *Dead Wrong: Violence, Vengeance and the Victims of Capital Punishment.* Westport, CT: Praeger, 2006.

Scott Turow — *Ultimate Punishment: A Lawyer's Reflections on Dealing with the Death Penalty.* New York: Farrar, Straus and Giroux, 2003.

Franklin E. Zimring — *The Contradictions of American Capital Punishment.* New York: Oxford University Press, 2003.

Periodicals

Bruce Anderson — "A Hanging Matter," *Spectator*, November 22, 2003.

Vince Beiser — "A Guilty Man: He Wanted to Make Capital Punishment Kinder," *Mother Jones*, September–October 2005.

Robert H. Bork — "Travesty Time, Again: In Its Death-Penalty Decision, the Supreme Court Hits a New Low," *National Review*, March 28, 2005.

William F. Buckley Jr. — "Spare Thoughts on Saddam," *National Review*, January 29, 2007.

Sara Catania   "Death Row Conversion: Traditional Opponents of Capital Punishment Have Gained Powerful and Unlikely Allies," *Mother Jones*, December 2005.

J. Daryl Charles   "Thoughts on Revenge and Retribution," *Touchstone*, December 2001.

Michael Cohen   "The Victims and the Furies in American Courts," *The Humanist*, January–February 2006.

Theodore Dalrymple   "'Barbaric!' They Charge: The Arrogance and Insularity of Death-Penalty Opponents," *National Review*, January 29, 2007.

Theodore Dalrymple   "The Meaning of Beheading: All Too Sad to Explain," *National Review*, October 24, 2005.

Aparisim Ghosh   "Saddam's Second Life," *Time*, January 15, 2007.

Ted Goertzel   "Capital Punishment and Homicide: Sociological Realities and Econometric Illusions," *Skeptical Inquirer*, July–August 2004.

Robert Grant   "Capital Punishment and Violence," *Humanist*, January–February 2004.

The *Economist* (U.S.)   "Here Is Thy Sting: Capital Punishment," April 28, 2007.

Cragg Hines   "There Should Be No Deadline for Justice," *Houston Chronicle*, October 2, 2003.

Jeff Jacoby

"When Murderers Die, Innocents Live," *Boston Globe*, September 28, 2003.

Alice Kim

"Death Penalty Exposed," *International Socialist Review*, March–April 2003.

Adam Liptak

"The Death Penalty Debate: The United States Is One of the Few Industrialized Nations that Still Uses Capital Punishment," *New York Times Upfront*, February 5, 2007.

Adam Liptak

"Death Penalty Losing Favor with U.S. Juries: Public Backs It, But Only in the Abstract," *International Herald Tribune*, May 23, 2007.

Dahlia Lithwick

"Fatal Retraction," *American Lawyer*, November 2003.

Patrick Mulvaney

"States Rethink Death Penalty as National Tide Turns," *National Catholic Reporter*, March 16, 2007.

Paul H. Rubin

"The Death Penalty and Deterrence," *Phi Kappa Phi Forum*, winter 2002.

Claire Schaeffer-Duffy

"Death Penalty Debate: As Connecticut's First Execution Since 1960 Draws Near, State's Bishops Urge Catholics to Speak Out," *National Catholic Reporter*, January 28, 2005.

Bruce Shapiro

"The Saddam Spectacle," *Nation*, January 22, 2007.

Clive Stafford Smith
"Forget the Statistics, Killing Is Wrong: Supporters of the Death Penalty Say It Deters Murderers," *New Scientist*, August 20, 2005.

Kathy Swedlow
"Forced Medication of Legally Incompetent Prisoners: A Primer," *Human Rights*, spring 2003.

William Tucker
"Deterring Homicides with the Death Penalty," *Human Events*, April 7, 2003.

Scott Turow
"To Kill or Not to Kill," *New Yorker*, January 6, 2003.

Tobias Winright
"Crime and Sacrifice: What Does the Cross Tell Us About the Ethics of Capital Punishment?" *Sojourners*, April 2007.

Benjamin Wittes
"The Executioner's Swan Song?" *Atlantic Monthly*, October 2005.

Lewis Yablonsky
"A Road into Minds of Murderers," *Los Angeles Times*, January 14, 2003.

Index

8